IMAGES
of Rail

THE BURLINGTON RAILROAD
ALLIANCE DIVISION

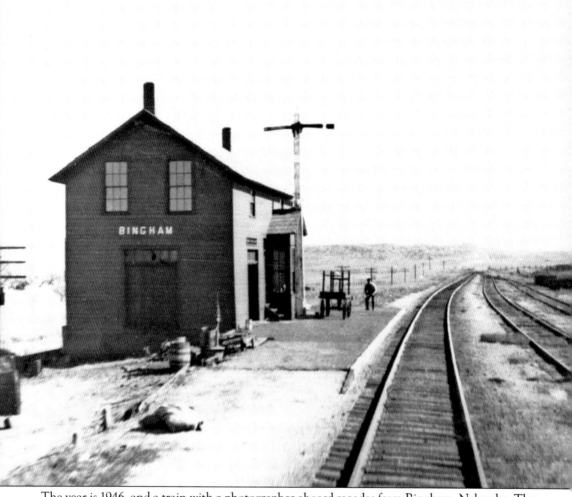

The year is 1946, and a train with a photographer aboard recedes from Bingham, Nebraska. The depot agent can be seen finishing up platform work at this remote Chicago, Burlington & Quincy Railroad outpost in the Nebraska Sandhills. The agent's position here was abolished prior to 1958. (J.C. Hardy, J.L. Ehernberger collection.)

ON THE COVER: Illustrative of how steam locomotives were very labor-intensive to maintain, a portion of the roundhouse and shop force at Alliance, Nebraska, posed with Chicago, Burlington & Quincy Railroad engine No. 312 on the roundhouse turntable in the early 1900s. Even the roundhouse mascot got in on the occasion! (Alliance Knight Museum.)

IMAGES
of Rail

THE BURLINGTON RAILROAD
ALLIANCE DIVISION

Richard C. Kistler, Michael M. Bartels,
and James J. Reisdorff

Copyright © 2014 by Richard C. Kistler, Michael M. Bartels, and James J. Reisdorff
ISBN 978-1-4671-1297-0

Published by Arcadia Publishing
Charleston, South Carolina

Printed in the United States of America

Library of Congress Control Number: 2014939282

For all general information, please contact Arcadia Publishing:
Telephone 843-853-2070
Fax 843-853-0044
E-mail sales@arcadiapublishing.com
For customer service and orders:
Toll-Free 1-888-313-2665

Visit us on the Internet at www.arcadiapublishing.com

*Dedicated to Joseph C. Hardy and his fellow
railroaders of the Alliance Division.*

Contents

Acknowledgments		6
Introduction		7
1.	Rails Create Alliance	9
2.	The Burlington in the Black Hills	27
3.	Alliance Division Territory	39
4.	Passenger Train Service	55
5.	Freight Train Service	65
6.	Motive Power	73
7.	Alliance Rail Facilities and Division Events	85
8.	The Burlington Northern Era	101
9.	The BNSF Era	117

Acknowledgments

As memories of the Chicago, Burlington & Quincy Railroad at Alliance fade with each passing year, and with corporate mergers creating a vastly different rail scene insofar as motive power, operations, and physical plant are concerned, a book like this is needed for what is perhaps a last, brief glance back at the one-time Alliance Division.

No one could have asked for a better experience than the one had by the authors in preparing this endeavor, allowing them the opportunity to touch base with those who helped in one way or another. Jim Ehernberger not only retrieved his own photographs, but made available images from the collections of others now in his possession. Hol Wagner furnished photographs from the Corbin/Wagner collection, while A.J. Wolff provided a number of his own photographs in addition to research on several matters that proved helpful. Thank you to Steve Snook for electronically scanning the bulk of the images appearing in this work, making final compilation much easier. Gratitude is extended to Jim Reese for his early efforts with the material, and to Becci Thomas and others at the Knight Museum and Sandhills Center in Alliance for assisting with images from the museum's collection. A big thank-you goes to Jerry Penry for his work in preparing an Alliance Division map. The Nebraska State Historical Society is acknowledged for assistance with photographs from the society's collection. Others who contributed their own photographs or ones from their collections include A.J. Holck, Ran Varney, Steve Snook, David Doering, and Travis Dewitz.

Additionally, appreciation is extended to the other photographers, known or unknown, living or deceased, whose images appear within as part of collections from other parties. And, finally, a posthumous thank-you goes to both Bernard G. Corbin and Joseph C. Hardy, noted historians of the Burlington Railroad. Their research, photography, and writings on the subject will allow their legacy to live on in perpetuity.

INTRODUCTION

During the last week of November 1889, the Burlington & Missouri River Railroad (B&MR) in Nebraska announced it was ready to ship coal from Newcastle, Wyoming, to various stations via its newly constructed line passing through the foundling railroad town of Alliance, Nebraska. Now, 125 years later, predominant among the abundance of traffic passing through Alliance on B&MR's modern-day successor, the BNSF Railway, are coal hoppers loaded with Wyoming or Montana "black diamonds" en route to power plants. As they snake across the plains, these coal trains give the appearance of a long string of dominoes, their symmetry contrasting with the natural beauty of such varied terrain as Nebraska's Sandhills and Wyoming's Wind River Canyon.

Alliance, originally named Grand Lake, became a rail center, or "division point," from its inception in 1888. (A railroad division point has historically been where train or engine crews are changed out in the course of train operations over a large segment of rail line, designated as a division. It has also historically been where facilities are maintained to service locomotives and railcars used on the division. Subsequently, a division point town was often the residency of large numbers of railroad employees needed for operating both the trains and service facilities.) In 1902, the importance of Alliance as a rail hub was reaffirmed when it became the headquarters of the railroad's Alliance Division, previously called the Wyoming Division. The B&MR would be merged into the Chicago, Burlington & Quincy, but for the next 67 years, much of the CB&Q's far west traffic would be under the control of the Alliance Division.

Much of the geography of the Alliance Division presented a challenge to the early railroaders operating trains across the division. For example, Crawford Hill, located 45 miles northwest of Alliance on the line to Edgemont, features nearly mountainous hills and valleys covered with trees and foliage. From an altitude of 3,791 feet at Alliance, the line gently climbs to Hemingford, Nebraska, at 4,208 feet, and then drops into the Niobrara River valley at Marsland, Nebraska, before scooting up to the state's highest elevation of 4,496 feet at Belmont, once the site of Nebraska's only railroad tunnel, atop Pine Ridge. The line then drops down a 1.5-percent ruling grade for 13 miles, with two horseshoe curves and numerous cuts, into the White River Valley at Crawford, elevation 3,678 feet.

In years past, the northern High Plains region had its windy solitude broken by the distant staccato of steam locomotives battling grades over Crawford Hill. Behind them were boxcars and stock cars in weathered hues of red, black tank cars filled with Wyoming oil, and flatcars stacked high with West Coast lumber moving circuitously eastward, allowing the lumber time to dry and brokers time to divert it as market demand dictated.

Within the vast area of the Alliance Division, the Burlington otherwise participated in the development of agriculture, animal husbandry, forestry, manufacturing, mining, and other ventures. This was accomplished through the company's aggressive traffic department, staffed by people knowledgeable as to what was good for the railroad and its domain. This included developing seeds that could germinate in arid areas having short growing seasons; bringing in herds of European cattle that could withstand the long, cold winters; and, in general, finding a wide variety of commodities for the company to haul.

Ranching was also an important industry to the Alliance Division. The Nebraska Stock Growers Association was founded in Alliance in 1889 to protect stockmen from illegal rustling. The Alliance Livestock Commission Company bought and sold market cattle locally until December 1976. Livestock operations abounded along the division, with most stations having a stockyard for cattle and sheep.

Passenger service on the Alliance Division was slow to develop, due in part to a slow expansion of the western territory served by the Burlington over a long period of time. However, the Burlington was quick to exploit not only the scenic beauty of the Black Hills, but also the therapeutic value of various thermal and mineral springs that gushed from the rocks, which many claimed could cure anything from an ingrown toenail to neurasthenia. After the B&MR extended a line to Deadwood, South Dakota, tourists had a choice of two routes to the town famed for frontier personalities like Calamity Jane. The first was to take a passenger train directly from Edgemont; the second was to travel to Newcastle, Wyoming, where tourists could detrain and board a specially built bus for a daylong trek through the hills. Other attractions in the region were accessible by train as well. Passengers could transfer to a branch line train that took them to Cody, Wyoming, which served as an entrance to Yellowstone National Park. Meanwhile, those riding accommodations between Lincoln, Nebraska, and Billings, Montana, could make a brief stop within sight of the Little Big Horn Battlefield in Montana and observe where George Armstrong Custer was defeated by Sitting Bull.

Cutbacks in rail service across the Alliance Division occurred as sources of revenue traffic dwindled and highways became more prominent. However, the Federal Clean Air Act of 1970 served as the stimulus that led to a new era for the Burlington. The act created interest in Montana and Wyoming low-sulphur coal, which became valuable because of an increased demand for electrical power coupled with the failure of nuclear power plant development. Western coal-mining activity by the Burlington in previous years had already resulted in the company having spurs built into area mines.

A new coal-hauling line began when the Amax Coal Company decided to develop a huge open-pit mine, Belle Ayr, southeast of Gillette, Wyoming. To serve it, the railroad in 1972 agreed to supervise construction of a long loop through a giant coal silo at its end. From a diverting point named Donkey Creek, after a nearby stream, on the Edgemont-Gillette subdivision, 18.2 miles of track were constructed in a southerly direction on a bed of shifting clay and a gradient that required helper engines. The Public Service Company of Colorado, from its Pueblo plant, delivered 110 solid-bottom, 110-ton coal hoppers that the Burlington ran on its first unit train to the mine. The Alliance Division's coal-train epoch was off and running.

Even after the CB&Q became part of the Burlington Northern in March 1970, the Alliance Division would serve as a designated part of the BN for another 18 years until it was abolished and split among other divisions on October 30, 1988. Yet, despite this loss of status, the Alliance community has continued to have its fortunes largely tied to the railroad that created it. Still another chapter opened on December 31, 1996, when Burlington Northern and the Atchison, Topeka & Santa Fe railroads merged into the Burlington Northern & Santa Fe Railway (BN&SF). Today, with its busy shop facilities and a seemingly continuous number of BNSF freight trains arriving and departing the community daily, the term "railroad town" is still very much part of Alliance's identity. The following pages illustrate how this status was achieved.

One

RAILS CREATE ALLIANCE

In the 1880s, building a railroad across the sparsely populated areas of central and western Nebraska, and into Wyoming, required substantial vision on the part of its promoters. This vision foresaw that the unbroken prairie traversed by such a rail line would someday see the establishment of towns, and, subsequently, the raising of crops and livestock that such a railroad could move to Eastern markets.

The Burlington & Missouri River Railroad (B&MR) and affiliates had built an extensive network south of the Platte River in Nebraska in the 1870s and early 1880s, but generally left the country to the north to the Union Pacific. However, completion of a 40-mile extension from Aurora to Grand Island on June 8, 1884, was seen as a prelude to a major push to the northwest. Speculation became a reality when the B&MR organized the Grand Island & Wyoming Central Railroad (GI&WC) on October 14, 1885. Kilpatrick Brothers & Collins of Beatrice, Nebraska, was contracted to build from Grand Island toward Wyoming and the Black Hills.

Construction from Grand Island commenced in December 1885, with the 100 miles to Anselmo, Nebraska, completed on September 12, 1886, and 99 additional miles to Whitman finished on May 30, 1887. Tracklayers arrived at what was known as Grand Lake on February 3, 1888. B&MR general superintendent George W. Holdrege suggested the site be renamed Alliance, which satisfied the need for a simple, one-word name. Platted by the Lincoln Land Co., a townsite company organized by Burlington officials but run as a separate entity, the new town incorporated in the summer of 1888, with buildings erected upon the open range. Just four years after its founding, Alliance had more than 1,000 people and boasted a US Land Office and, most important, a division headquarters for the B&MR west of Ravenna.

Construction resumed west from Alliance in November 1888. The goal now was coal, a good vein having been discovered north of Newcastle, Wyoming. The line opened for business to the western border of South Dakota, west of Dewey (formerly the S&G Ranch) on November 18, 1889. South Dakota had gained admission as a state 16 days earlier. With few towns established beyond Crawford, Nebraska, Siding No. 7, which was located 54 miles west of Crawford, became Edgemont, South Dakota, in the spring of 1890. Construction here included a depot and railroad yard. Edgemont would be the terminus for B&MR construction only briefly. The push toward Gillette, Wyoming, and that region's coal reserves soon began.

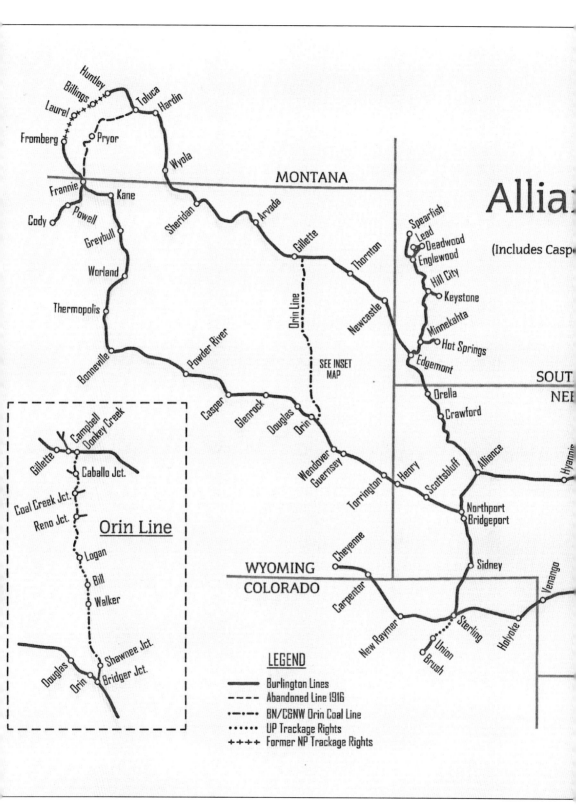

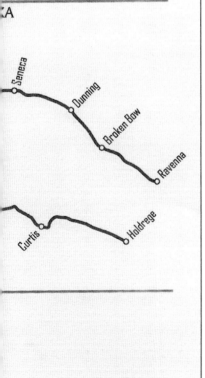

This map specifically made for this book shows the Alliance Division at about the height of its operations, covering Burlington Railroad operations in five states just east of the Rocky Mountains. (Not shown is territory that Alliance briefly operated in the 1960s when it controlled rail operations around McCook, Nebraska, which included branch lines in Kansas.) At its peak in the Chicago, Burlington & Quincy Railroad era, Alliance maintained control over a sprawling territory with a variety of revenue traffic. Branch lines north from Edgemont, South Dakota, into the Black Hills provided outlets to minerals and lumber. Coal mines near Newcastle, Wyoming, provided the railroad with fuel sources for its own locomotives as well as for customers. Oil and open-range livestock came from around Casper, Wyoming. Meanwhile, the areas around Scottsbluff, Nebraska, and Sterling, Colorado, were known for their annual fall rush of sugar beet traffic. (Map by Jerry Penry.)

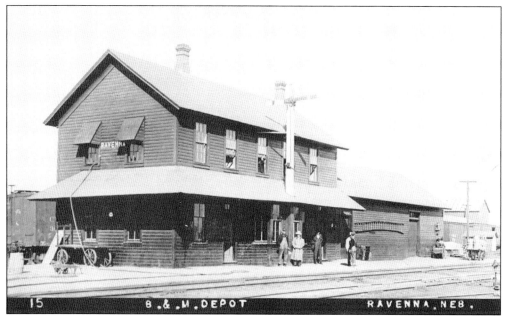

Although Ravenna station belonged to the Lincoln Division, it was the starting point for the Alliance Division's main line to Edgemont. The original Ravenna depot was constructed in 1886 and remodeled in 1914. Note the crooked ladder on the freight house wall and the hose running into the upstairs window. (J.L. Ehernberger collection.)

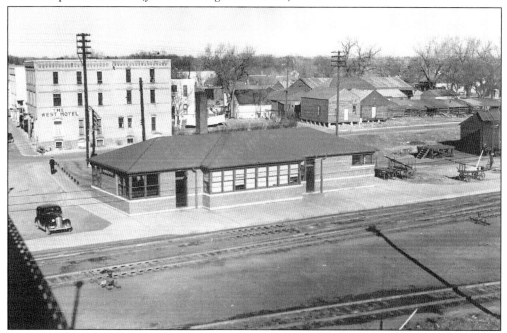

Replacing the original frame station, an attractive brick depot was constructed at Ravenna in 1945. It is pictured here on December 14, 1946. In turn, this structure was razed on May 10, 1982, after being replaced by a new office building. Burlington Northern received permission in March 1984 to close its Ravenna agency, with operators and clerk positions remaining for a time at this crew change point. (J.C. Hardy, J.L. Ehernberger collection.)

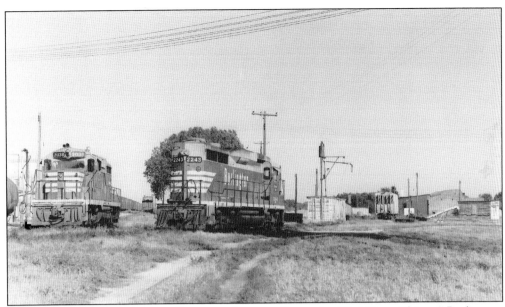

The Ravenna service area was still a tranquil spot on September 25, 1971, as Chicago, Burlington & Quincy Railroad (CB&Q) GP20 No. 2038 and GP40 No. 2243 wait assignment. The coal-train era had just begun, and Ravenna would never be the same. (J.L. Ehernberger photograph.)

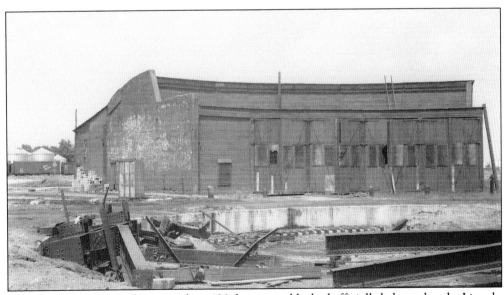

Ravenna's 10-stall roundhouse, with its 100-foot turntable, had officially belonged to the Lincoln Division. However, it also serviced Alliance Division power, which turned here. By July 7, 1961, the date of this photograph, the facility had long been idle. Scrap from the turntable laid about for several years. (A.J. Holck.)

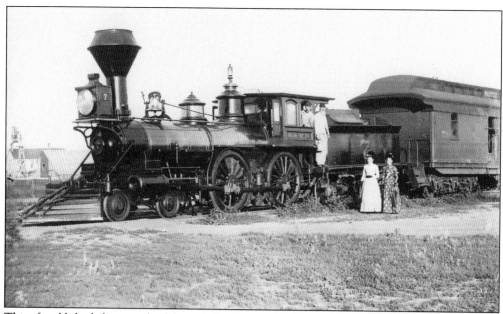

This oft-published photograph of the early Burlington & Missouri River Railroad in Nebraska shows 4-4-0 No. 7, the *Wauhoo*, with its cab crew and two female admirers at Broken Bow, Nebraska, around 1887. Steam locomotion was a driving force behind settlement of the Sandhills region in the 19th century. (Solomon Butcher, Nebraska State Historical Society collection.)

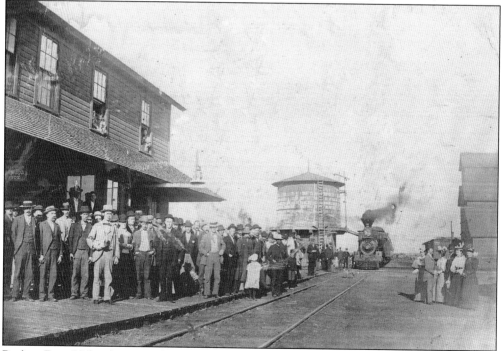

Broken Bow, Nebraska, 48 miles west of Ravenna, became a station on the Grand Island & Wyoming Central Railroad. What prompted this large turnout at the Broken Bow depot, around 1890, is no longer known. A diamond-stacked locomotive is having its water replenished prior to continuing its journey with a passenger train. (R.D. Varney collection.)

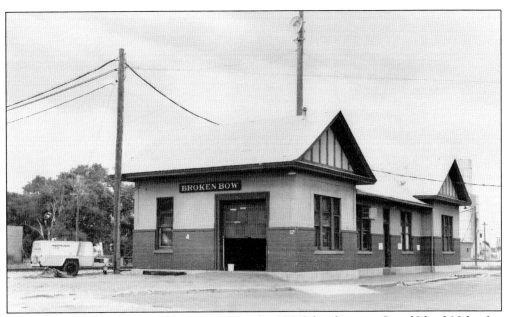

Broken Bow developed into the largest city along the CB&Q line between Grand Island, Nebraska, and Alliance. This brick-stucco depot, built in 1916, served the town until the end of passenger service. Broken Bow's station agency was closed on August 29, 1986, but the depot continues to serve maintenance-of-way personnel. (Corbin/Wagner collection.)

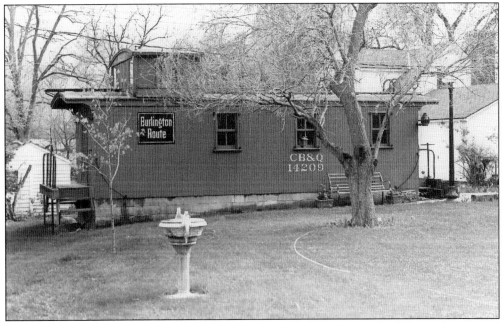

Alliance Division conductor Art Gordon logged about 4,500 miles a month while traveling aboard CB&Q caboose No. 14209 in the early 1900s. After suffering a job injury in 1905, Gordon gave up railroading and worked as a Merna, Nebraska, druggist for many years. He acquired No. 14209 from the CB&Q in 1950 and placed it in his backyard as a popular social clubhouse. Grace Varney later moved the 14209 to Broken Bow for a similar use, where it is pictured in 1984. The 14209 is now a recreational cabin near Arnold, Nebraska. (J.J. Reisdorff.)

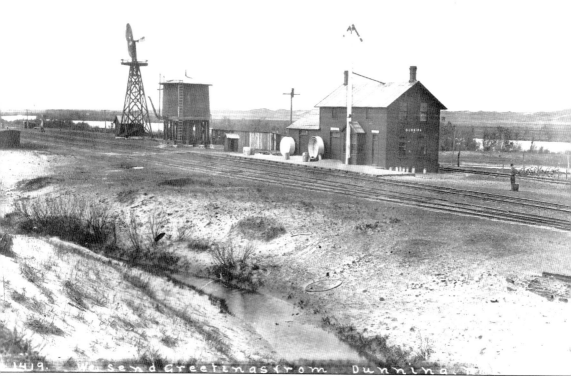

Station facilities at Dunning, Nebraska, were typical of those dotting the Burlington & Missouri River's line through the Nebraska Sandhills region. Dunning, with a peak population of 450 around 1910, had been platted by the Lincoln Land Company. Here, a lone passenger patiently awaits his train. A tornado on August 6, 1908, partially damaged this structure. It was later destroyed in a fire resulting from the collision of a train and a gas truck near the depot on October 9, 1944. A temporary structure then served until the agency closed in 1959. (J.L. Ehernberger collection.)

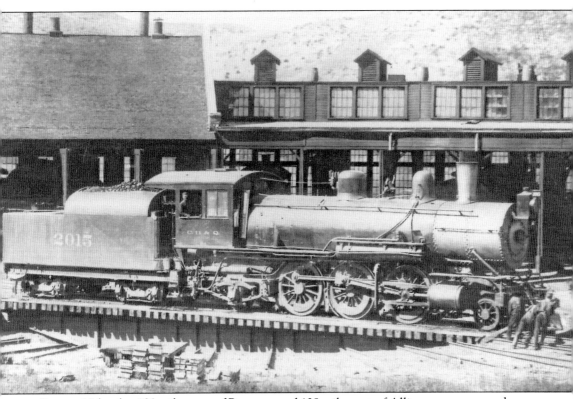

Seneca, Nebraska, 130 miles west of Ravenna and 108 miles east of Alliance, was a crew change point for freight trains until August 1, 1973, when Alliance-Ravenna run-throughs began. Here, three men heave into the Armstrong turntable at the Seneca roundhouse around 1909. The foreman watches their progress in rotating R4 No. 2015, the largest engine the 70-foot table could handle. It was replaced in 1918 by a 90-foot, electric-powered table. The five stalls at left were the original 1888 B&MR brick construction, while the five frame stalls at right were added in 1907. The entire roundhouse was razed in 1940, subsequent to locomotive runs being lengthened in the mid-1920s and Seneca being eliminated as a change-out point. (J.L. Ehernberger collection.)

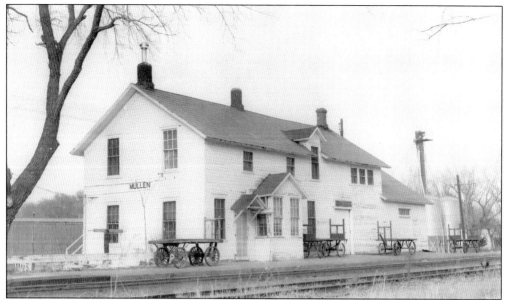

Mullen, Nebraska, was named for Charles D. Mullen, chief clerk to B&MR division superintendent D.E. Thompson. The Mullen depot, a two-story frame building with attached freight room, stands out in recently applied white paint on February 18, 1968. The 1912 structure was later replaced with a one-story frame depot moved here from Ashby, Nebraska. The agency was discontinued in 1982. (Corbin/Wagner collection.)

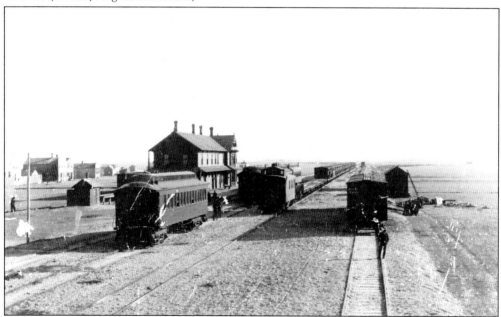

Alliance, Nebraska, lies west of the Sandhills on a high, treeless tableland. This early view of the Alliance depot and yards shows the western Nebraska town to be "just a wide spot on the open prairie." An eastbound freight indicates that the cattle business here was already well established. The first Alliance depot, a 12-foot-by-18-foot shed, was ready for use on February 3, 1888. The first regular train arrived a month later. Seen here is the second depot, a two-story frame structure built in 1888 at the foot of Box Butte Avenue. (Alliance Knight Museum.)

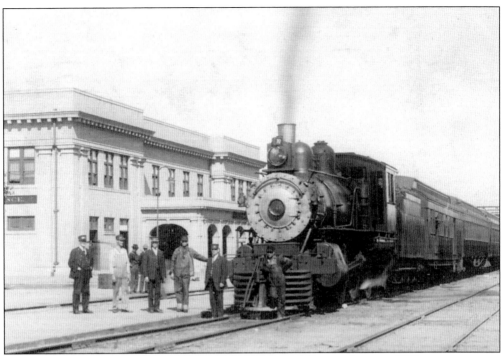

A westbound passenger train stopped at the nearly new Alliance depot in 1909, its crew posing next to K4 type No. 717. This 4-6-0, constructed at the Havelock Shops in 1902 as Burlington & Missouri River Railroad No. 64, served in both freight and passenger service on the Alliance Division. (Hol Wagner collection.)

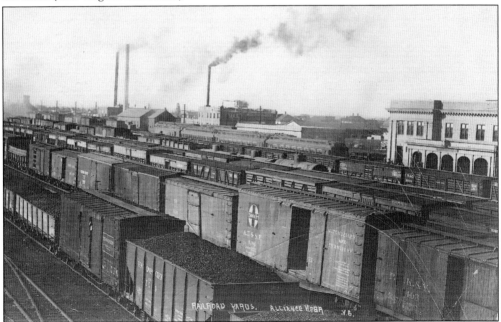

Cars of various types from other railroads fill the Alliance yard tracks in this 1925 postcard view, indicating the large volume of traffic handled here. Visible to the left of the depot are several passenger cars of the era. (Hol Wagner collection.)

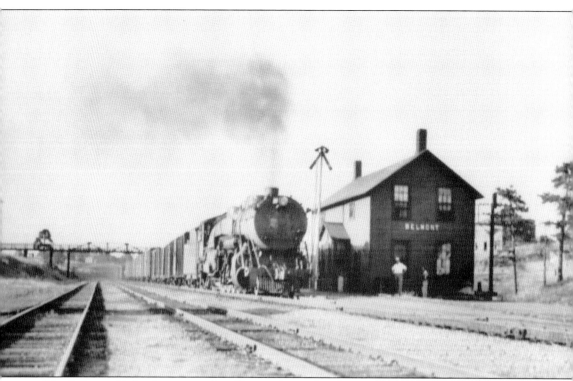

The Belmont, Nebraska, train order office was located at the top of Crawford Hill. From Belmont, the dispatcher at Alliance could reach trains on the Hill, providing new orders for helper engines or stopping trains if needed. In this undated photograph, a 6100 series 2-10-2 blasts past the Belmont depot with eastbound tonnage while the agent and his wife look on. For westbounds, the elevation between Marsland, Nebraska, and Belmont increased 333 feet in nine miles. Eastbounds faced an 813-foot rise within the 13 miles from Crawford, Nebraska, to Belmont. When automatic signals were installed after World War II, Belmont was reduced to a daytime shift. It closed entirely in 1955 after helpers were issued return orders at Crawford. (J.L. Ehernberger collection.)

Nebraska's only railroad tunnel was located north of Belmont. This early view shows the south end of the 713-foot bore constructed at the crest of a 1,000-foot incline. Building the tunnel took two years, with about 600 men using mules and dump carts. Dynamite helped carve the tunnel out of compacted sand and butte rock. The construction firm Kilpatrick Brothers & Collins finished the project on August 18, 1889. A 20-car livestock train was the first through the bore. The original timbers used in the Belmont tunnel were replaced in the 1920s, when it was re-bored and concreted. (Alliance Knight Museum.)

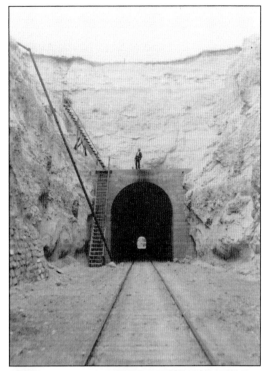

Passenger train No. 43, with E8 No. 9949A, paused at the north portal of the Belmont tunnel on July 31, 1966, so that railroad enthusiasts on board could record the view. On the tail end of No. 43 this day was the Pullman observation car *Cornhusker Club*, then privately owned. (F.H. Bahm, J.J. Reisdorff collection.)

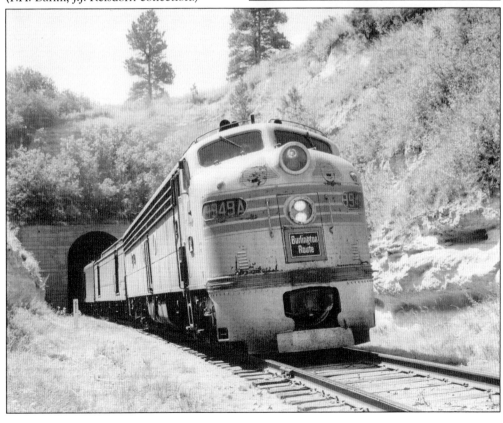

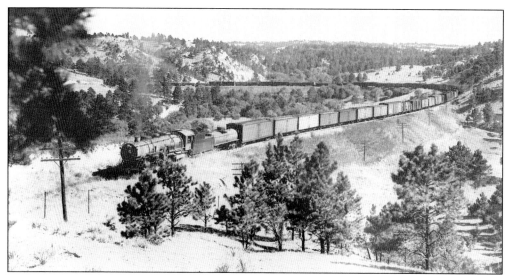

In the mid-1940s, amid the beauty of the Pine Ridge area of Nebraska, 2-10-2 No. 6155 pulls a freight train over Horseshoe Curve, just north of Belmont. The tanker behind 6155 was an auxiliary water car, then standard equipment for steam on Alliance-Edgemont runs. Straight across from 6155, ahead of the train's caboose, was another 2-10-2 pushing its share of the load over Crawford Hill. (Corbin/Wagner collection.)

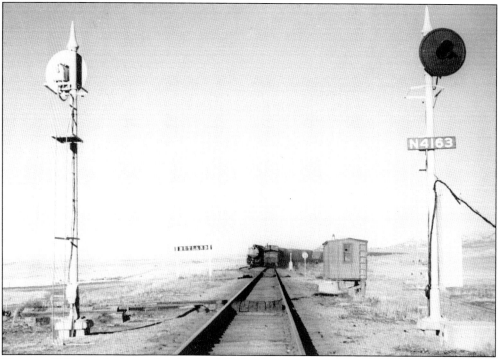

This rare 1946 view looks north at Rutland, Nebraska, a station siding midway between Belmont and Crawford. In the distance, two freight trains pass each other. During World War I, the car body at right had served as a 24-hour train order office. The Burlington later removed the siding as an economy measure, only to replace it in the coal traffic years. (J.C. Hardy, J.L. Ehernberger collection.)

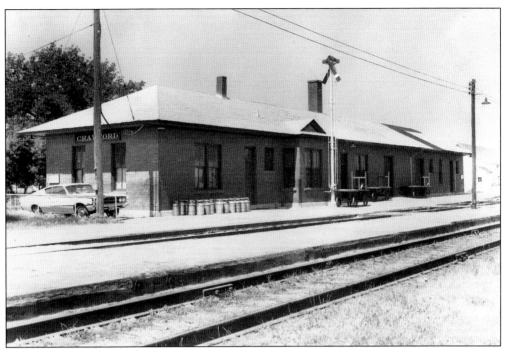

Crawford was once a busy station, with 24-hour operators on account of helper service, plus interchange with the Chicago & North Western (C&NW). An interlocking tower at the CB&Q-C&NW crossing here was removed in the 1930s. A frame depot, which burned down in 1912, was replaced by a 24-foot-by-138-foot brick depot. Depicted here on June 29, 1968, this depot was razed in 1988. (Corbin/Wagner collection.)

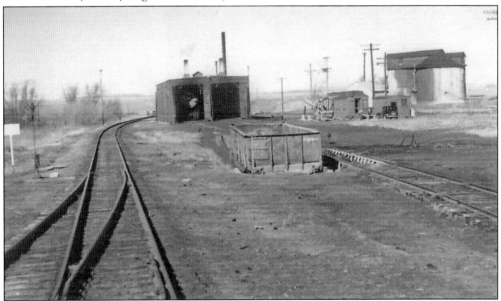

A two-stall engine house at Crawford, Nebraska, was used for locomotives in helper service out of here. Seen while in use on November 6, 1948, both stalls were 128 feet long. Note the gondola parked below ground level at the locomotive cinder pit, which aided in loading cinders. (J.C. Hardy, J.L. Ehernberger collection.)

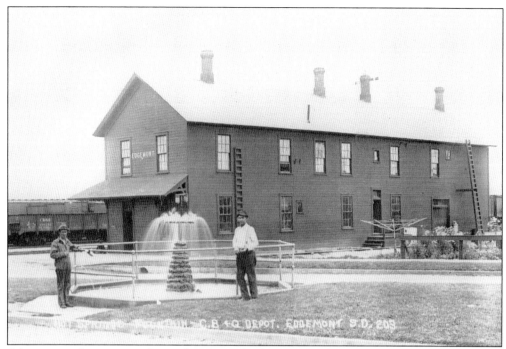

A hot springs fountain was featured in the park adjoining the depot at Edgemont, South Dakota. The depot's second floor contained a dispatcher's office. It later became a layover room for passenger train crews. This building had its second story removed in the 1950s, and was demolished altogether in 1979, replaced by a modern BN-era office structure. (Corbin/Wagner collection.)

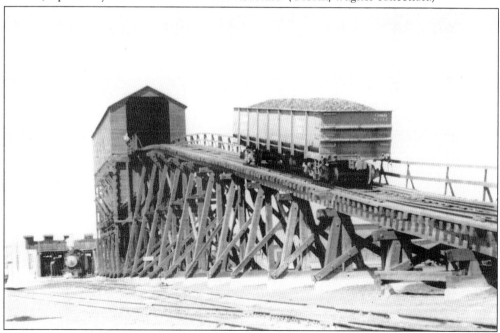

Edgemont's car-pull coaling ramp and dock are shown here in the late 1920s. A fully loaded 40-foot Burlington gondola is being pulled up the ramp by cable as a worker watches from the top. (Corbin/Wagner collection.)

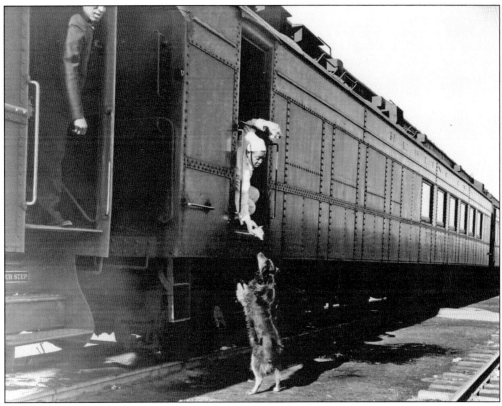

A collie named Brownie was the "railroad dog" of Edgemont. He was generally found in the cozy comforts of the train order office, where his canine license prominently hung on the wall. However, handouts from the dining car chef on train No. 43 would find Brownie trackside. The collie never had trouble locating the diner's galley door, as seen here on April 3, 1949. (J.C. Hardy, J.L. Ehernberger collection.)

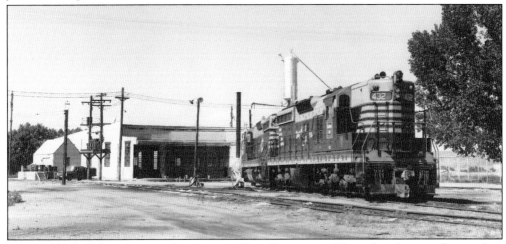

At its peak, the Edgemont roundhouse was a 20-stall structure. When this photograph was taken on July 9, 1967, five stalls of the Edgemont house, painted white, remained. The turntable was still available if needed. CB&Q SD9s Nos. 432 and 342 are parked next to a newly installed sanding tower. (J.L. Ehernberger photograph.)

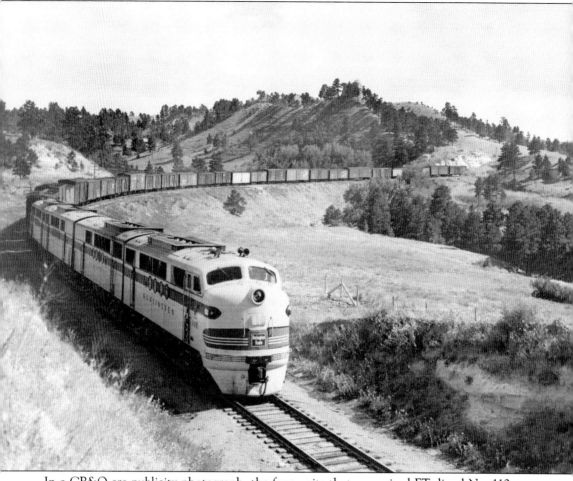

In a CB&Q-era publicity photograph, the four units that comprised FT diesel No. 110 were wrapping freight train No. 80 around Horseshoe Curve while en route to Lincoln, Nebraska. The 5,400-horsepower diesels, built in 1943–1944, gave excellent performance in freight service. However, it would be another six years before diesels purged steam from most freight assignments on the Alliance line. (Corbin/Wagner collection.)

Two

The Burlington in the Black Hills

The historic and resources-rich Black Hills region of southwestern South Dakota was once part of the Burlington Railroad's Alliance Division. However, the last portion of a once-extensive Burlington track system that served the Hills area was abandoned in 1986, two years prior to the end of the Alliance Division.

Discovery of gold in the Black Hills in 1874 sparked a major mining boom, although outside rail connections would not arrive for another 16 years. Chicago & North Western's Fremont, Elkhorn & Missouri Valley reached Deadwood late in 1890, just ahead of the Burlington & Missouri River's Grand Island & Wyoming Central on February 1, 1891. Branches were completed to Hot Springs in 1891, Spearfish in 1893, and Keystone in 1900. The Burlington also acquired two narrow gauges, the Black Hills & Fort Pierre and the Deadwood Central, that had been developed as local railroads before outside connections were available. Both CB&Q and C&NW would operate narrow-gauge systems in the Hills, with the Q even providing electric interurban passenger service. Connections were available at Mystic to Rapid City via the 34-mile Rapid City, Black Hills & Western Railroad until it was abandoned in 1947.

Cutbacks took place as sources of ore, minerals, and lumber were depleted and early highways were constructed. The Q's narrow-gauge interurbans were discontinued in 1924, followed by the demise of all narrow-gauge operations in 1930. The Spearfish branch was abandoned in 1934 after flood damage. The deadly Black Hills flood of June 9, 1972, washed out the last mile of the Keystone branch, forcing BN to truck out stranded cars and build a new runaround track to the west. The tourist-hauling Black Hills Central shifted its operations to Hill City–Custer before returning to the Keystone branch in 1977 and buying it in 1981.

Coal traffic slowed the demise of the Edgemont-Deadwood line, as the Black Hills Power & Light plant at Kirk continued to get large quantities of fuel. By the early 1970s, traffic consisted of a triweekly local, with trips to Hot Springs and Keystone as needed. With low traffic and trestles in poor condition, the Hot Springs spur was abandoned in 1977. Service ended between Custer and Deadwood in 1983 and between Edgemont and Custer in 1986. The 109 miles from Edgemont to Deadwood were made into the George S. Mickelson Trail, completed in 1998. It honors the late South Dakota governor who supported its creation.

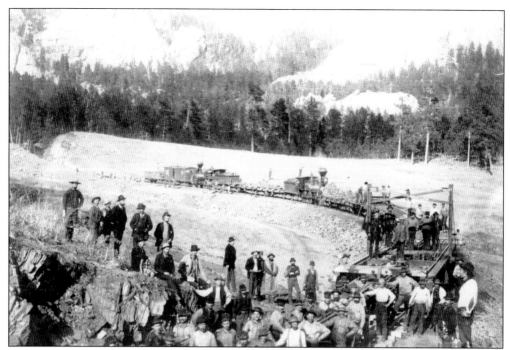

Grand Island & Wyoming Central tracklayers pause for the photographer while completing a horseshoe curve opposite the Blue Horn Mountains near Custer, South Dakota, around October 1890. B&MR 4-4-0s Nos. 156 and 149 power the construction train as it progresses north through the Black Hills. (Corbin/Wagner collection.)

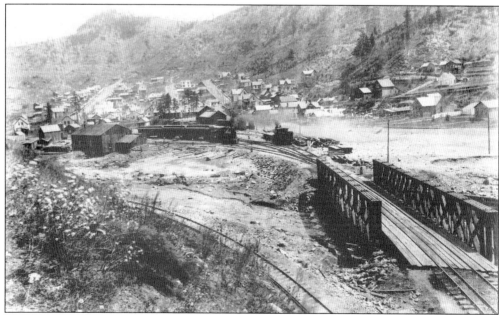

The south end of the yard at Deadwood, South Dakota, is shown here around 1900, with the Burlington's afternoon passenger train leaving for Edgemont. The wooden bridge seen here was later replaced by a steel span. When a narrow-gauge CB&Q interurban line from Deadwood to Lead began service in 1902, an overhead wire was installed. (E.F. King, R.C. Kistler collection.)

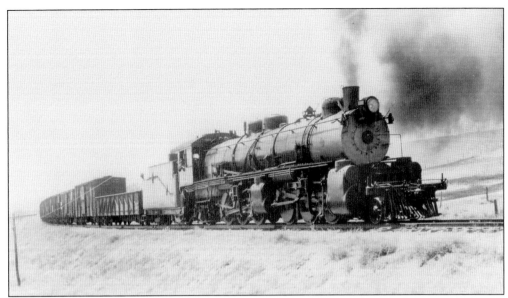

The CB&Q's huge T2 class Mallet-type locomotives once moved freight as well as passenger trains over the Edgemont-Deadwood line. Built in 1910, all 10 served in the Black Hills at various times between 1910 and 1952. Seen here thundering around a curve after leaving Edgemont on June 20, 1936, the 4105 was assigned to Alliance between 1923 and 1950. This engine later served as a pusher at Bridgeport, Nebraska, in the late 1940s, assisting northbound freights up Angora Hill. (Otto C. Perry, J.L. Ehernberger collection.)

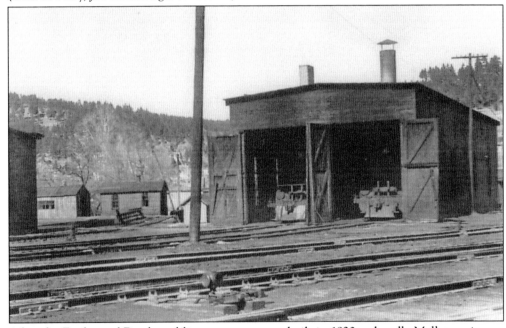

After the Englewood-Deadwood line segment was rebuilt in 1930 to handle Mallet engines, a two-stall Mallet shed was erected in Deadwood and the Mallets worked into there. Here, two T2-type 2-6-6-2s are stored neatly inside the Deadwood Mallet shed on March 16, 1948, awaiting assignment back to Edgemont. This shed was later restored as part of historic Deadwood. (J.C. Hardy, J.L. Ehernberger collection.)

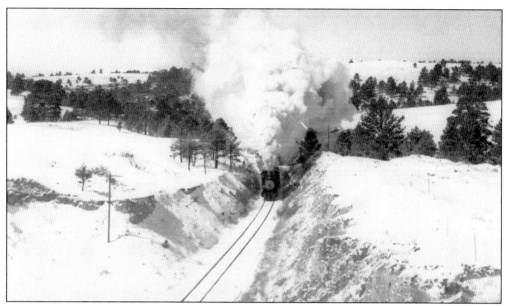

When air-conditioned, all-steel Denver-Deadwood coaches were added to trains 141 and 142, they were too heavy for the CB&Q's 10-wheeled engines to handle. The CB&Q then borrowed heavier 10-wheelers from its subsidiary line, the Colorado & Southern. These engines came to the Deadwood branch in 1931. Here, one of the C&S engines blasts along near Chilson, South Dakota, with train 141 on a wintry day in February 1948. (J.C. Hardy, J.L. Ehernberger collection.)

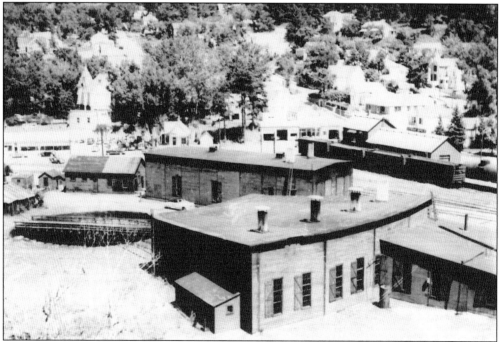

A view from July 3, 1951, shows the roundhouse and turntable at Deadwood, along with the Mallet shed and freight house. The attached shed on the roundhouse sheltered both an 0-6-0 switcher and the 4-6-0 off trains 141 and 142. It had previously housed narrow-gauge power for the Deadwood Central. (J.C. Hardy, J.L. Ehernberger collection.)

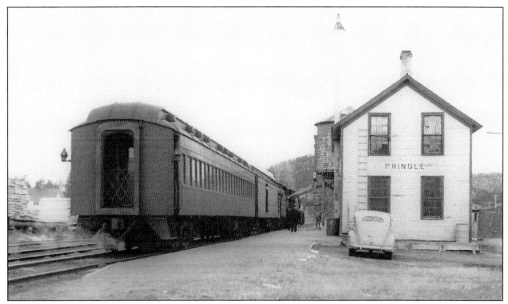

The Burlington's Deadwood branch local 141 takes on water at Pringle, South Dakota, as mail, baggage, and express are transferred on April 27, 1949. The water at Pringle was soft and pure, requiring no treatment for locomotive boiler use. (J.C. Hardy, J.L. Ehernberger collection.)

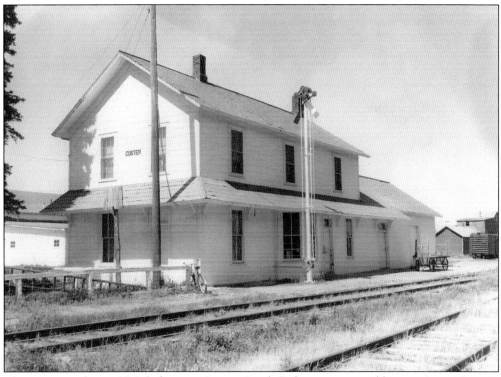

The two-story frame CB&Q depot at Custer, South Dakota, is pictured here on June 25, 1966, the 90th anniversary of Lt. Gen. George Armstrong Custer's defeat by Native Americans at Little Big Horn in Montana. This structure was identical to the depot at Hill City. Custer's depot had been sold and removed by mid-1982. (Corbin/Wagner collection.)

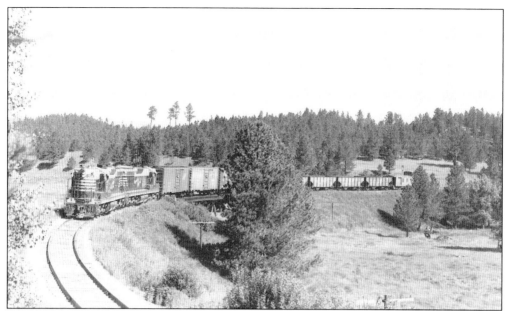

CB&Q SD9s Nos. 354 and 350 negotiate a curve above milepost 65 near Hill City, South Dakota, on July 10, 1967. This triweekly mixed train, carrying passengers and freight, had replaced regular passenger service in late 1949. (J.L. Ehernberger photograph.)

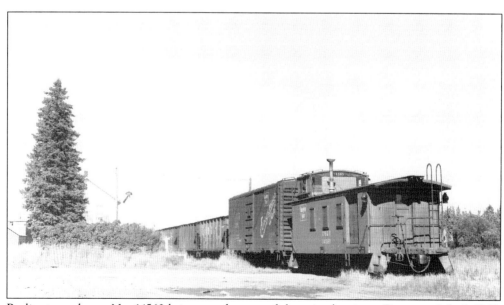

Burlington caboose No. 14560 brings up the rear of the mixed train at Custer on July 9, 1967, en route to Deadwood. Ridership in the old side-door accommodation was then infrequent. (J.L. Ehernberger photograph.)

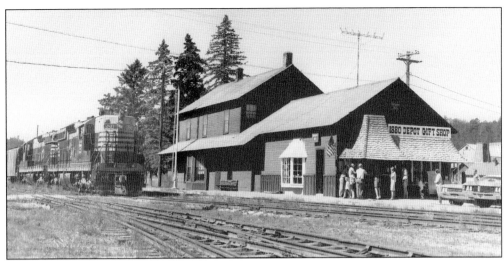

The Black Hills Central Railway (BHC) has been a steam tourist line in service over a portion of the Burlington since 1957. It started operations between Hill City and a station called Oblivion. In cooperation with CB&Q, five miles of the Keystone branch were third-railed to accommodate the first BHC engine, a three-foot-gauge 2-8-0. A second BHC train began in 1962, using a standard-gauge 2-6-2 from an Arkansas short line. Narrow-gauge operations ended after 1964. Here, SD9 No. 350 rolls past the Hill City depot, adapted for BHC excursion service, on July 10, 1967. Since the BHC then operated over CB&Q-owned tracks, a CB&Q operator was employed at BHC expense to handle train orders. (J.L. Ehernberger photograph.)

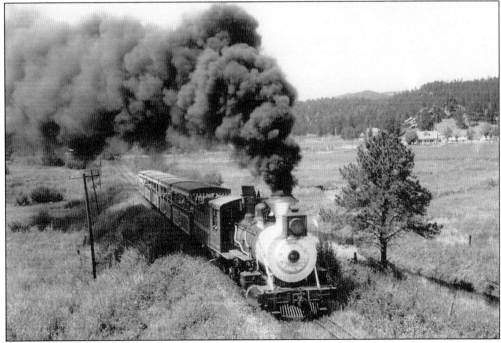

Engine No. 69 gives Black Hills tourists a ride on the Burlington's Keystone branch in August 1964. This narrow-gauge 2-8-0 had originally been used on the White Pass & Yukon Railway (WP&Y) in Alaska. No. 69 was later used on two separate tourist lines in Nebraska. In 2005, No. 69 was taken back to Alaska in order to again operate on the WP&Y. (Hol Wagner.)

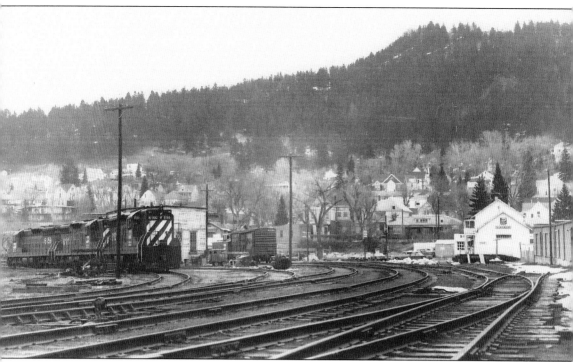

With limited space, the Burlington's rail yard at Deadwood had to be fitted to optimize every available square foot of land. Seen here on April 16, 1975, are three SD9s (left) and the freight depot (right). The remaining yard tracks curved left toward the former passenger depot site. Following the demise of passenger service into Deadwood, the station agency moved to the freight house, which served as a depot until it was closed by BN on June 28, 1975. (J.L. Ehernberger photograph.)

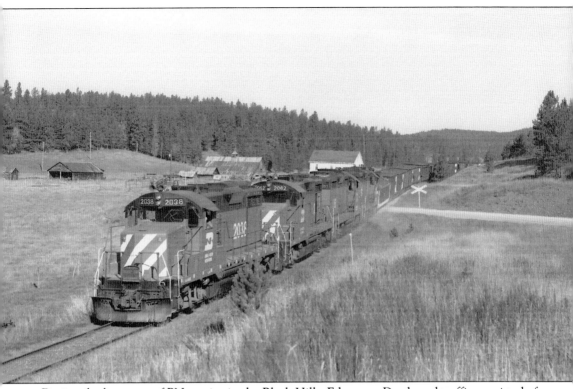

During the last years of BN service in the Black Hills, Edgemont-Deadwood traffic consisted of a triweekly local, with trips to Hot Springs and Keystone on an as-needed basis. Here, the BN's local for Edgemont, South Dakota, rolls through the countryside near Dumont, South Dakota, on September 15, 1981. GP20s replaced SD9s as motive power on the Deadwood run in early 1983. Here, four GP20 locomotives handle empty coal hoppers from Kirk. These 2,000-horsepower units held the Custer-Deadwood assignment until the line was abandoned. (A.J. Wolff.)

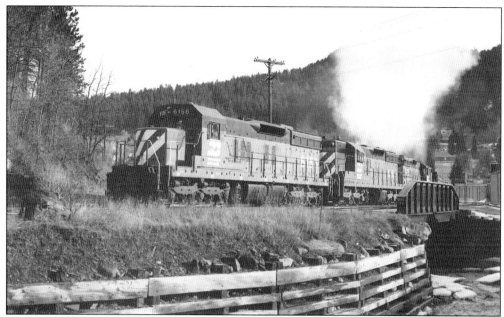

Chop-nosed SD9 No. 6158 heads up a southbound train departing Deadwood on the morning of February 19, 1980. For this trip, four motors provided 7,000 horsepower for train 856. Frequently, 12 hours were insufficient to complete the run when side trips over the Keystone and Hot Springs spurs were required. (A.J. Wolff.)

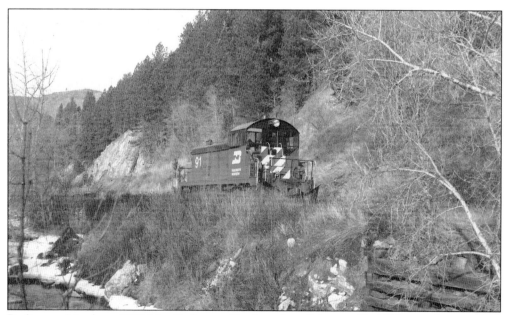

Burlington Northern SW1 No. 91 departs Deadwood on February 10, 1980, in order to switch the Black Hills Power & Light plant at Kirk, South Dakota. The local from Edgemont dropped off coal loads at Kirk, with the switcher then spotting empties for the local to pick up on the way from Deadwood. (A.J. Wolff.)

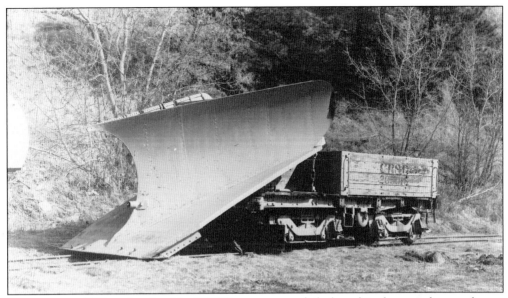

The services of BN wedge plow No. 205618 were not needed when this photograph was taken at Deadwood on April 16, 1975. The undercarriage of this abbreviated snow fighter consisted of the frame and trucks off the tender of CB&Q 2-6-0 No. 1056. Steep grades necessitated this type of plow. It was later retired by BN. (J.L. Ehernberger photograph.)

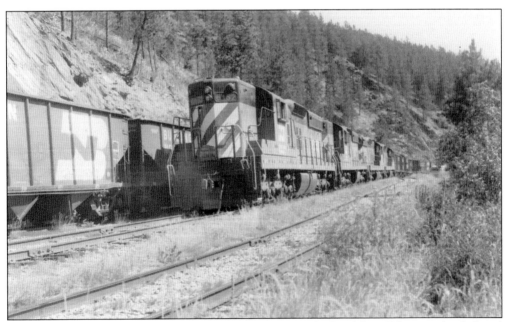

On August 4, 1980, four SD9 units switch at Yates Spur. The local from Edgemont hauled coal loads north to Kirk, South Dakota, for Black Hills Power & Light, while the southbound train returned the empties from Kirk, using Yates as a holding yard. BN continued service until the power plant at Kirk contracted for delivery of coal by truck from Black Hills Power's Wyodak coal mine near Gillette, Wyoming. (J.R. Douda.)

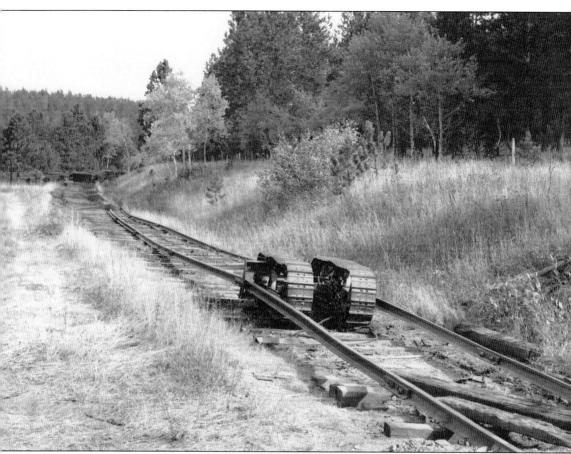

Burlington Northern's abandonment of the 65.7-mile Custer-Deadwood segment was approved by the Interstate Commerce Commission, effective October 15, 1983. The last High Line train departed Deadwood on November 8, 1983, with the last switcher at Deadwood moved dead in train. The aftermath is depicted at Dumont, South Dakota, five miles south of Englewood, on September 21, 1984. A crawler-type apparatus with side brackets effectively pulled rail up from the ties as it was advanced by a cable attached to a tractor. Traffic south of Custer was then limited to shippers at Lien and Custer. Finally, in 1986, BN discontinued the Edgemont-Custer line, as business was no longer sufficient to maintain service. (A.J. Wolff.)

Three

ALLIANCE DIVISION TERRITORY

As the Burlington's western territory expanded, it became necessary to create additional crew districts, engine service, and dispatch centers in order to efficiently operate these lines. From Edgemont, South Dakota, the Burlington continued northwest into Wyoming under the name of the Grand Island & Northern Wyoming Railroad. It reached Gillette on August 12, 1891, and Sheridan on November 26, 1892. In 1894, it was pushed on to connect with the Northern Pacific at Huntley, Montana, east of Billings, forming a through route to the Pacific Northwest. In 1901, a 129-mile branch was completed from Toluca, Montana, to Cody, Wyoming, gateway to Yellowstone National Park. This territory had been known as the Wyoming Division, but on December 1, 1902, it was split at Newcastle, Wyoming, becoming the Alliance Division to the east and the Sheridan Division to the west.

Union Pacific's inaction let the Burlington stake first claim to the North Platte River Valley, completing lines in 1900 from Alliance to Guernsey, Wyoming, and from Northport, Nebraska, to connect with its Chicago-Denver main line at Brush, Colorado. At Sterling, Colorado, it crossed the Burlington's High Line from Holdrege, Nebraska, to Cheyenne, Wyoming. Sterling would also become a division headquarters in October 1904.

In 1901, the Great Northern and Northern Pacific acquired 98 percent of the Burlington's stock. In 1908, the CB&Q in turn acquired control of the Colorado & Southern. A new route built southeast through central Wyoming would open a shorter route to Denver and the Gulf of Mexico. The first segment, from Frannie to Greybull, Wyoming, was completed in 1906. Service was extended to Casper on October 20, 1913, and on August 28, 1914, a connection was made with the C&S at Orin Junction. These lines were placed under the new Casper Division in 1914.

The need for economy reduced the number of divisions. The timetable of March 29, 1953, reflected the merger of the Sterling Division with Alliance. The latter had already handled dispatching since the early 1930s when the Sterling office was closed. Effective May 3, 1953, the Sheridan Division merged with Casper. On October 30, 1960, all divisions combined into Alliance under one superintendent, and with Alliance handling all dispatching. More territory was added on March 1, 1969, when the McCook Division was split up between the Lincoln and Alliance Divisions.

By July 1980, Alliance was the largest of 15 operating Burlington Northern divisions. Its total ton-miles and train-miles for coal shipments surpassed that of some other major railroads then operating in the United States.

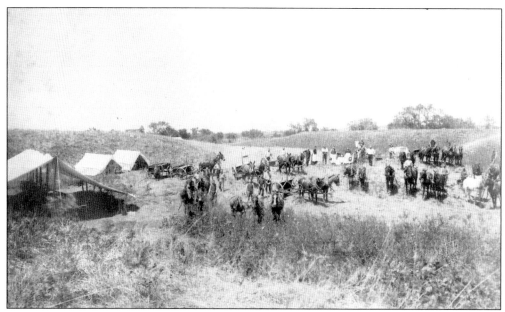

The R.C. Flins railroad-grading outfit took time out for this photograph while working near Newcastle, Wyoming. A note on the original print remarked on this being fine grazing country occupied by thousands of head of cattle. The date of the photograph is not known. (J.L. Ehernberger collection.)

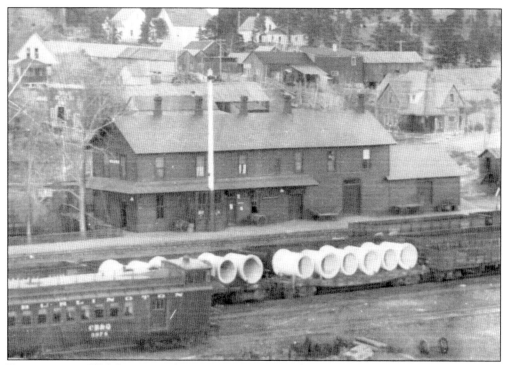

For many years, CB&Q trains and engine crews terminated at Newcastle rather than at Edgemont, South Dakota. The original five-chimney frame depot at Newcastle reflected its status as a division point structure. It is pictured here in April 1919. (J.L. Ehernberger collection.)

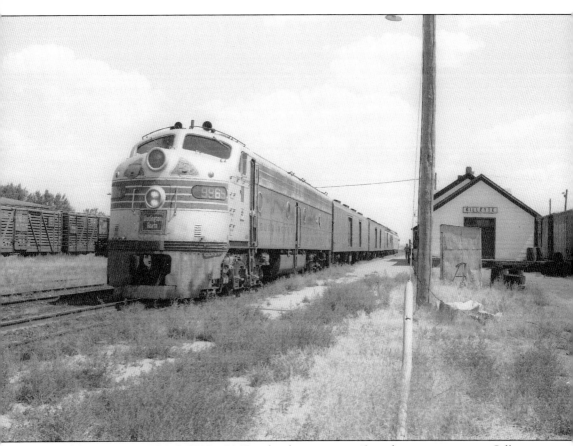

Bound for Montana, CB&Q E8 No. 9965 with a four-car train 43 made its station stop at Gillette, Wyoming, on August 13, 1967. The 2,000-horsepower diesel, built in 1952 by EMD, was standard power in later years on Alliance Division passenger trains. Gillette, for some reason, never received a modern depot of brick or stone construction to replace the old two-story frame structure (right). This was despite the fact that Gillette was a terminal employing continuous-duty operators and clerks. In addition, Gillette was a larger town than some that did acquire better station facilities. (F.H. Bahm, J.L. Ehernberger collection.)

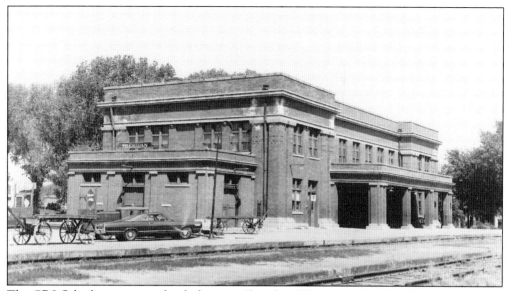

The CB&Q built a two-story brick depot at Sheridan, Wyoming, in 1911. The original frame depot was then remodeled into a freight house. This 55-foot-by-128-foot boxlike structure, seen here on August 13, 1967, was designed similar to the Alliance passenger depot. Sheridan Division headquarters were upstairs, with the attached structure at left having served as the Railway Express Agency office. Today, in the BNSF era, operating and engineering staff utilize the facility. (J.L. Ehernberger photograph.)

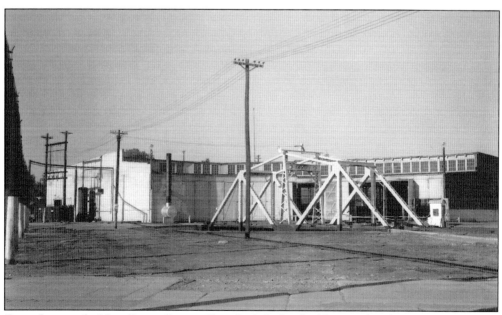

Once the site of a 25-stall roundhouse, Sheridan's facility had been reduced to nine stalls by the time the photographer came by on July 30, 1963. A 100-foot turntable was still in service here. (A.J. Holck.)

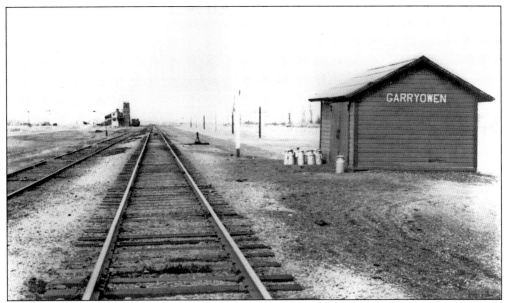

Garryowen, Montana, pictured in 1945, was then a flag stop on the Billings line. "Garryowen" was the regimental song for George A. Custer's 7th Cavalry. The Little Big Horn Battlefield, where Custer and about 200 of his men were killed in 1876 while fighting Native American warriors, is located nearby. At one time, passenger trains paused at a platform near the battlefield to allow passengers to view the area. (Corbin/Wagner collection.)

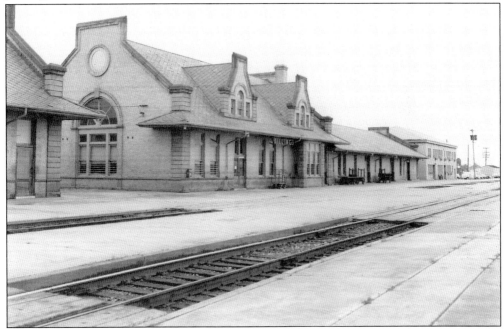

Constructed by Northern Pacific in 1908, three stone buildings comprised the station facility at Billings, Montana. CB&Q passenger trains used this facility until 1969. Dispatchers, trainmasters, and other staff were located in the office building at right. This photograph was taken on August 3, 1972. Local preservationists later succeeded in renovating the station, which now serves as a community center. (Corbin/Wagner collection.)

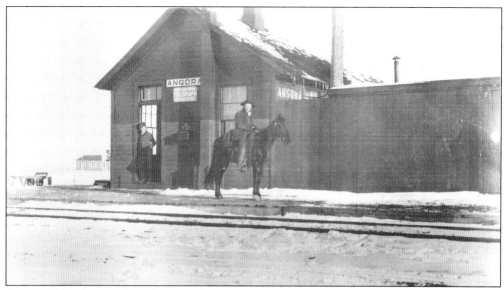

Angora, Nebraska, was the only manned station between Alliance and Northport, Nebraska. Helpers were required on northbound loaded trains to ascend Angora Hill. This undated photograph of the first depot shows a small shack with a dismounted boxcar attached for use as a freight house. Meanwhile, the agent is following company rules by wearing proper attire on duty. It appears the horseman is ready to dispatch letter mail to nearby residents. (J.L. Ehernberger collection.)

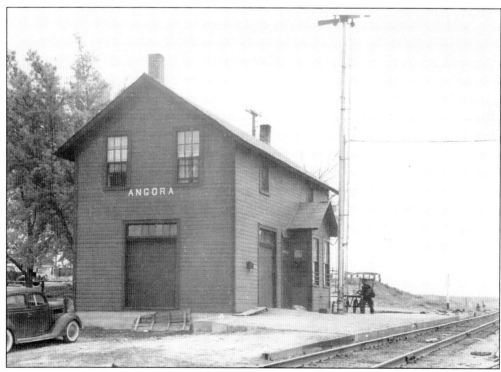

In contrast to the depot shown above, this more adequate, two-story frame "Burlington saltbox" served as the Angora depot when this photograph was taken in 1948. Regulatory permission to close the agency here was granted in May 1961. (Corbin/Wagner collection.)

Northport, Nebraska, was the crossing of Union Pacific's O'Fallons–South Torrington branch and the Burlington's Alliance-Sterling line. For CB&Q, Northport was a place name only, equipped with a telephone, wye track, and small yard. CB&Q station facilities were located at Bridgeport, 2.73 miles south. Northport's interlocking tower, seen here in the early 1900s, was owned and operated by UP. The velocipede, with spouted oil can sitting in a tray, was used by the operators to fill oil-burning lamps in nearby railroad signals. Rods emerging from the foundation indicate the tower was hand-operated. This tower closed in 1933, replaced by an automatic interlocking plant. (J.L. Ehernberger collection.)

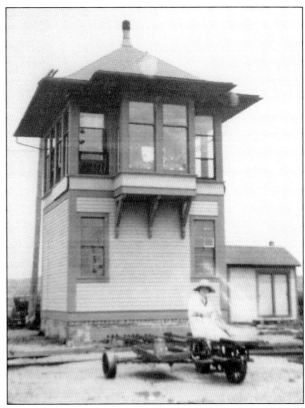

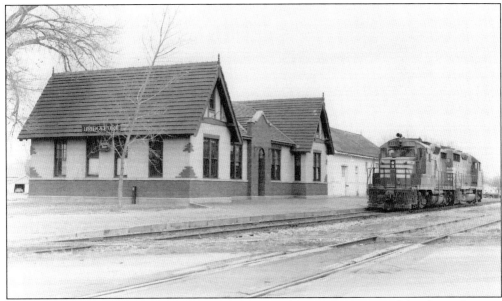

In 1929, the CB&Q erected a picturesque brick-stucco depot at Bridgeport, Nebraska, replacing a frame structure. GP20 No. 933 and mate are shown alongside the building on December 20, 1969. Closed in November 1983, this depot still serves in the BNSF era. Long gone is a 150-ton coal chute erected here in 1922, along with water cranes used to service steam engines. The former roundhouse here was later used by an agricultural facility. (J.L. Ehernberger photograph.)

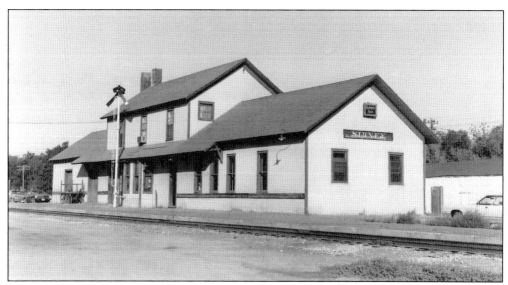

Sidney, Nebraska, is where the Burlington crosses over the UP's Council Bluffs–Cheyenne main line. The frame depot here, originally built as the CB&Q depot at Sterling, Colorado, was moved to Sidney around 1907. It was enlarged and had stucco applied in 1924. Pictured in August 1971, the Sidney depot was closed on March 14, 1986. It was one of the last depots in Nebraska with an agent who resided in the second-floor living quarters. (J.L. Ehernberger photograph.)

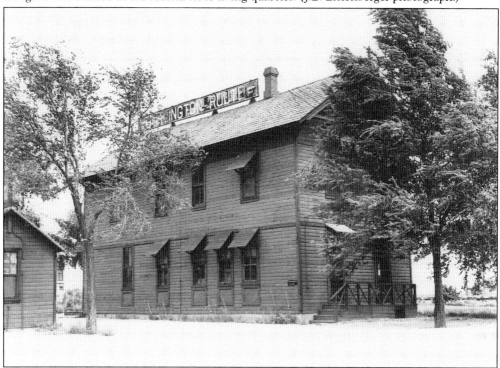

The CB&Q's office building at Sterling, Colorado, had been moved there on a flatcar from Holyoke, Colorado, around 1907. Pictured here on August 9, 1949, it then housed an assistant superintendent and a roadmaster. It was one of the few division offices on the Burlington system to be housed in a frame structure by that date. (J.C. Hardy, J.L. Ehernberger collection.)

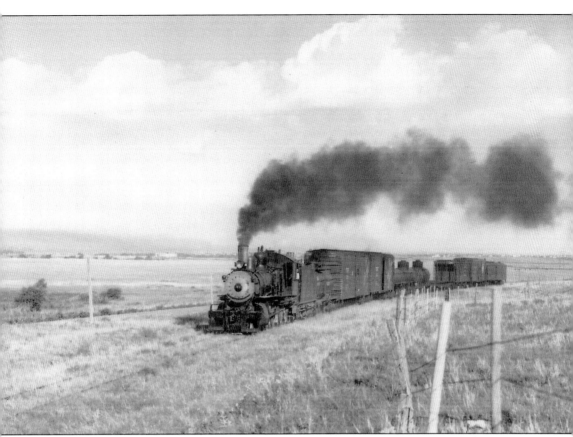

Rail photographer Jim Ehernberger's interest in the Burlington's Cheyenne-Sterling branch line began early enough for him to record the last use of steam on that line. Here, mixed train 159, west of Altvan, Wyoming, was making the last westward trip using CB&Q 4-6-0 No. 919 on August 3, 1956. This locomotive would later be placed on historic display at Alliance. (J.L. Ehernberger photograph.)

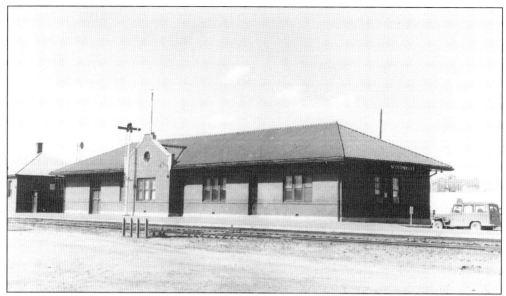

Scottsbluff, Nebraska, was the largest town on the Burlington's North Platte Valley line east of Wendover, Wyoming. Increased business required construction in 1917 of a new brick passenger station, freight house, and coaling station at Scottsbluff. The separate freight house is visible at left in this photograph from April 6, 1967. This line produced a considerable amount of revenue from seasonal sugar beet shipments. (J.L. Ehernberger photograph.)

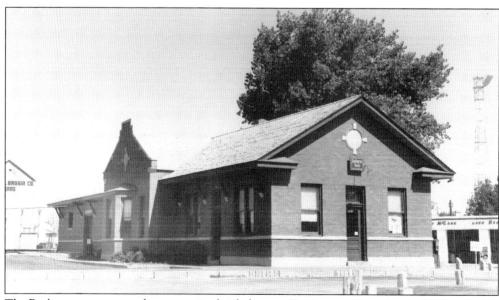

The Burlington constructed an attractive brick depot at Torrington, Wyoming, in 1928, replacing an earlier frame building. However, by July 9, 1967, when this photograph was taken, the depot's neat appearance was a moot point, since passenger service had ended the previous year. Torrington's operator position was eliminated on March 12, 1981, upon completion of the Alliance-Guernsey Centralized Traffic Control system. The depot was later razed, and the site was used for a fast-food restaurant. (J.L. Ehernberger photograph.)

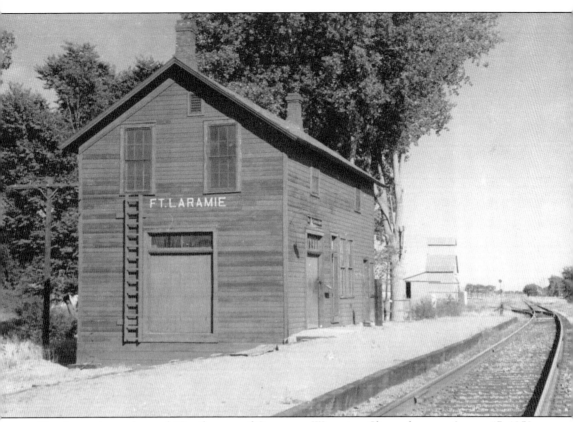

Fort Laramie was located 13 miles east of Guernsey, Wyoming. Shown here on August 17, 1958, is the Fort Laramie depot. The agency had been discontinued prior to this date, but this station continued as a train order office until February 28, 1981, when the East Guernsey CTC system was activated. The depot was later moved a short distance for private use. Old Fort Laramie, first established as a trading post, was sold to the government in 1849 and converted into a military post to protect travelers on the Oregon Trail. It also served as a relay point for the Pony Express. Remains of the fort are now a historic site. (Corbin/Wagner collection.)

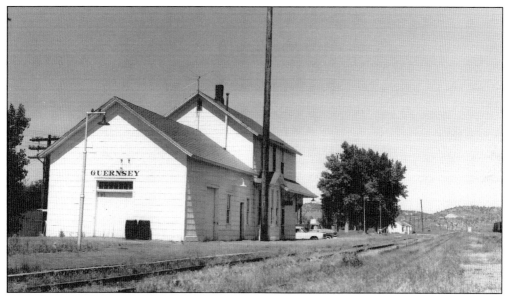

Everything appears tranquil at Guernsey on July 9, 1967, prior to the onslaught of coal traffic that would materialize in this region within a few years. At this time, Guernsey had an agent in addition to first-, second-, and third-shift operators, allowing for continuous 24-hour operation. (J.L. Ehernberger photograph.)

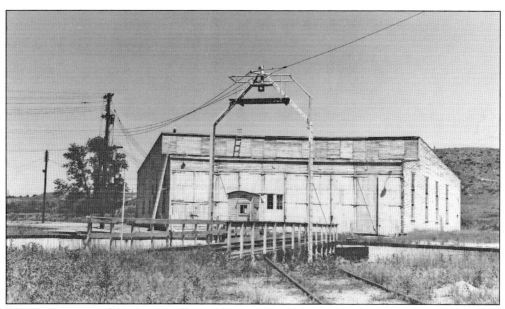

The Guernsey roundhouse originally consisted of 10 stalls, each 100 feet. Like the roundhouse at Bridgeport, Nebraska, this structure was equipped with a 100-foot turntable. By July 9, 1967, the Guernsey structure had been reduced to five stalls. (J.L. Ehernberger photograph.)

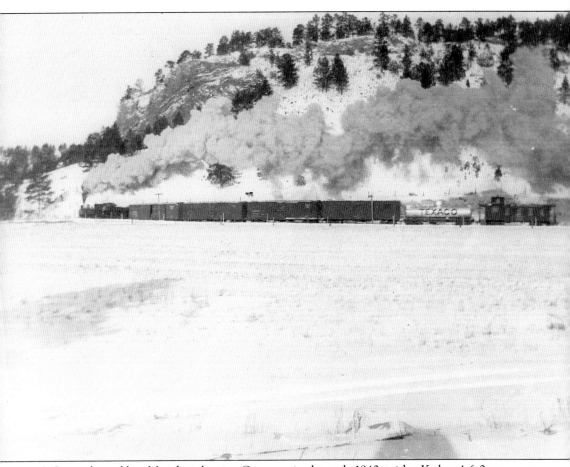

A Casper-bound local freight is leaving Guernsey in the early 1940s with a K-class 4-6-0 as power. A Texaco tank car was regular fare for every freight in and out of Casper. On account of the terrain immediately west of Guernsey, this train would go underground for part of its trip. The first tunnel was 1.9 miles west of the depot at milepost 96.85, a second tunnel was located at milepost 98.14, and a third was at milepost 101.47, all three within a 4.62-mile stretch. Tunnel No. 2 was daylighted in 1998 as part of BNSF improvements. (Corbin/Wagner collection.)

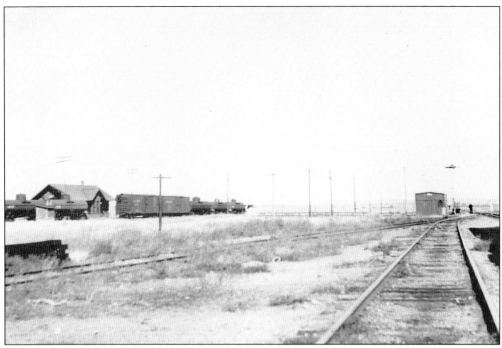

This 1947 view looking eastward at Orin, Wyoming, shows the Chicago & North Western depot (left) aside the railroad's Lusk-Douglas main line. The diagonal track served as a transfer track, with the CB&Q siding (right) for meets. A shed for mail and express sits aside the CB&Q's Guernsey-Billings line. The C&NW agent-operator handled business for both roads and could operate the CB&Q train order signal from the C&NW depot. (Corbin/Wagner collection.)

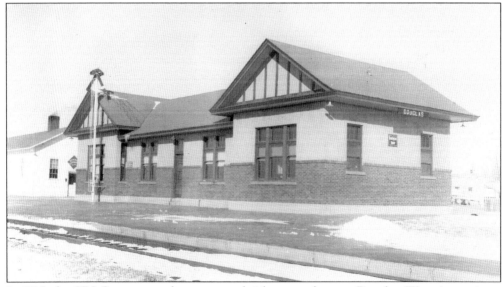

In 1915, the CB&Q constructed a one-story, brick-stucco depot at Douglas, Wyoming, using a design similar to several other Burlington depots built during this period. This facility replaced an earlier frame structure. Winter had already come to Douglas when this photograph was taken on October 31, 1961. The depot here remains in BNSF service. The town is now otherwise the site of the Douglas Railroad Interpretive Center, a large rail museum. (Corbin/Wagner collection.)

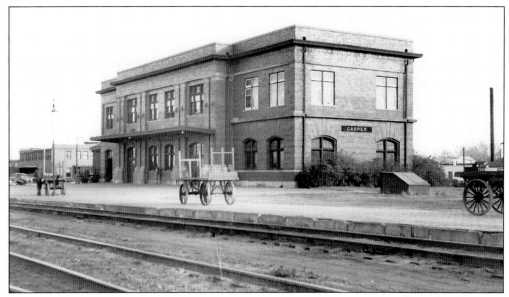

The two-story CB&Q depot and Casper Division headquarters at Casper, Wyoming, was constructed in 1915. Pictured here on October 26, 1947, the upper floor had offices for the superintendent, trainmaster, roadmaster, and dispatchers. When the Sheridan Division combined with Casper, an assistant superintendent was retained at Sheridan. This structure remains in service for BNSF personnel. A roundhouse had also been located here, consisting of 20 stalls at its peak. Only 10 stalls remained by 1959, with an 85-foot turntable. (J.C. Hardy, J.L. Ehernberger collection.)

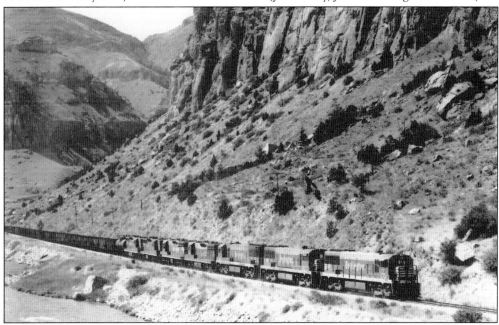

CB&Q daily freight 77, operating from Casper to Laurel, Montana, passes through Wind River Canyon on September 9, 1968. Trains 77 and 78 moved a considerable amount of traffic to and from Denver, in addition to North Platte Valley line business. It appears that plenty of power has been assigned to this train. Boulders that make up portions of the canyon wall have proven hazardous to rail traffic. (J.L. Ehernberger photograph.)

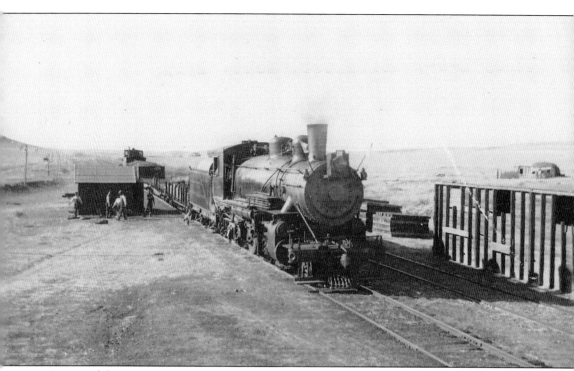

As one of the more remote sections of track once controlled by the Alliance Division, Extra No. 2219 was stopped at Wellfleet, Nebraska, on the treeless plains of Lincoln County, in 1915. Despite the appearance of the area, the region was a good revenue producer for the CB&Q from hauling grain and livestock. The R5 Prairie-type engine was then standard power on the Sterling-Holdrege subdivision. (Hol Wagner collection.)

Four
Passenger Train Service

Since most early Western railroads had little competition for passenger service, companies like the Burlington sometimes offered as little and as poor-quality transportation as they could. A Lincoln-Billings passenger train each way, 41 and 42, initially sufficed in this sparsely settled territory. But by the early 1900s, another train set, 43 and 44, had also been extended to Billings. A third pair, locals 39 and 40, ran as far west as Broken Bow or Seneca until 1928. The through trains continued west of Billings to Seattle via the Northern Pacific and Great Northern into the early 1920s, with through sleeping cars continuing into the 1950s. As late as 1956, a car operated between Omaha and Great Falls, Montana. Sleeping cars were also carried to Cody, Wyoming, for Yellowstone visitors through the 1953 season. Trains 31 and 32 between Alliance and Casper, Wyoming, had a through sleeper from Omaha, and a second train was added between Alliance and Denver in 1910.

The Great Depression saw trains 43 and 44 downgraded to motors or mixed trains before service was upgraded in 1936. Trains 42 and 43 became the Vacation Special, later the Adventureland, and 41 and 44 the General Custer. Wartime demands to conserve transportation resources cut Alliance-Denver service in half on September 24, 1942, and eliminated 41 and 44 west of Edgemont, South Dakota, on December 10, 1942.

The Adventureland name was dropped in 1948, and diesels began arriving in 1947, but Alliance Division trains never achieved Zephyr status. Streamlined sleeping cars appeared in 1959, but the Omaha-Billings car was dropped in 1960 and the Omaha-Casper car was cut back to Alliance on September 10, 1962. That same year, the Alliance-Casper café coach was discontinued, as was the diner out of Alliance on train 43 that was handed off to 42 at Ulm, Wyoming. Trains 41 and 44, now just a Lincoln-Alliance local, were discontinued on March 7, 1960. The last runs were made between Alliance and Casper on February 28, 1966, and between Alliance and Denver on July 7, 1967. Denver-Billings trains 29 and 30 made their last departures on September 1, 1967. Only 42 and 43 remained between Omaha and Billings, but they would leave on their last trips, too, on August 24, 1969, after a hard-fought discontinuance battle.

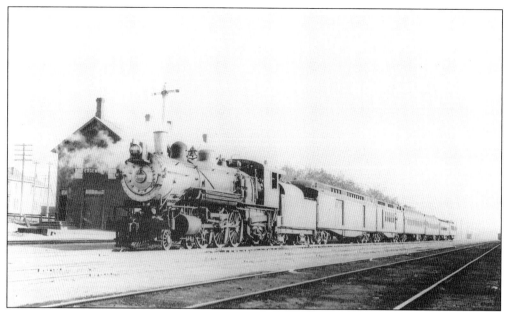

Train 44, the Southeast Express, makes a station stop and crew change at Edgemont, South Dakota, in 1922. This full-service train also carried a Deadwood-Lincoln Pullman. The café-parlor car was placed on train 10 at Lincoln, Nebraska, for Chicago, while the remainder of the consist went to Kansas City. Class engine No. 2900, only 12 years old, was assigned to mainline passenger service. (J.F. Adams, Corbin/Wagner collection.)

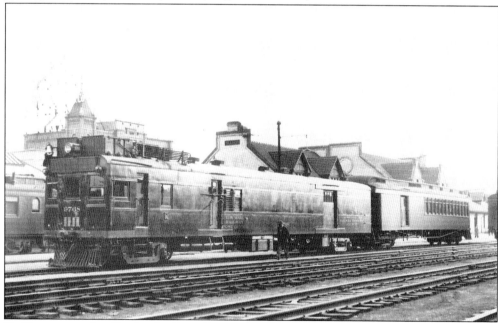

Traffic revenues, hard hit by the Great Depression, forced the CB&Q to reduce Lincoln-Billings trains 43 and 44 to motorcar service between Edgemont, South Dakota, and Billings, Montana. As conditions worsened, the motor, in January 1933, was carded to run Ravenna-Billings, a distance of 713 miles! This became the longest motorcar run on the CB&Q system. Train 43 is seen here at Billings on May 11, 1933. (Otto Perry, Corbin/Wagner collection.)

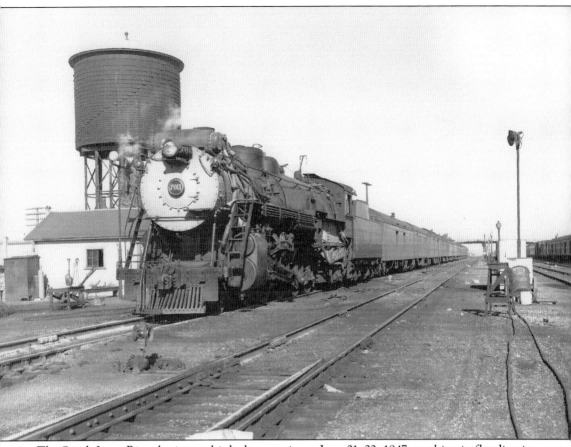

The South Loup River basin was hit by heavy rain on June 21–22, 1947, resulting in flooding in the area of Ravenna, Nebraska. A total of 14 miles of CB&Q right-of-way was severely damaged between Litchfield and Ravenna, with service finally restored on July 6. Burlington trains en route from Alliance were handed to the UP at Sidney, Nebraska, to detour around the flood-damaged segment, returning to the Ravenna-Lincoln main at Grand Island to continue their trip east. A reversal of this process was utilized for westbound traffic. Here, CB&Q train 43, with B1A No. 7011 on point, was stopped at North Platte, Nebraska, while detouring over the Union Pacific on June 28. (A.E. Stensvad, A.J. Holck collection.)

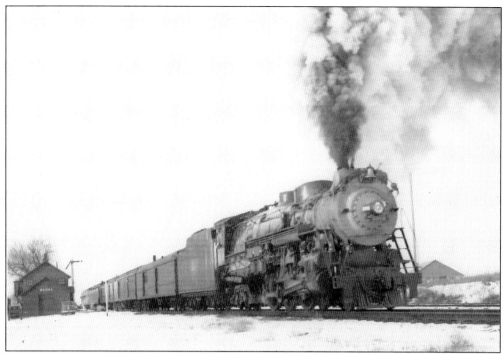

Trains 43 and 44 provided a vital link for Nebraska Sandhills residents, offering daily service. Ready to depart Merna, Nebraska, on January 2, 1948, train 44 is being hauled by S4A No. 4000. This 4-6-4 type, originally built in 1930 as the 3002, was rebuilt in 1937 to the 4000, with a streamlined shroud. It was then named *Aeolus*, "Keeper of the Wind." The streamlined shroud came off in early 1942. (F.G. Gschwind, J.L. Ehernberger collection.)

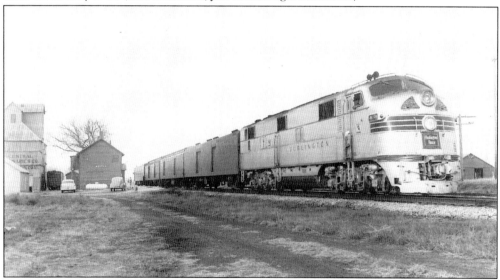

On November 20, 1955, the photographer was again at Merna for the station stop of train 44. Standard motive power on Alliance passenger assignments in the CB&Q diesel era seemed to be E7s. The engineer on 44 is looking back for the signal that will tell him the mail transfer is completed. He will then accelerate the 2,000-horsepower engine of No. 9922-A toward the next stop. (F.G. Gschwind, J.L. Ehernberger collection.)

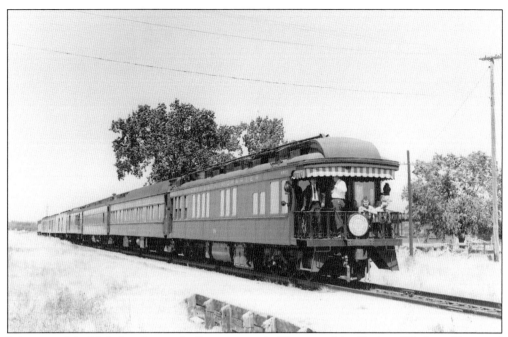

Private car No. 96, belonging to the Intermountain Chapter of the National Railway Historical Society, brings up the rear of train 43 at Provo, South Dakota, on August 2, 1964. Upon arrival at Edgemont, this observation car was removed for an excursion up the Deadwood branch. This car was ex-CB&Q (second) No. 96, built in 1886. Acquired by Intermountain in 1962, it was retired and placed on display at the Colorado Railroad Museum in 1972. (J.L. Ehernberger photograph.)

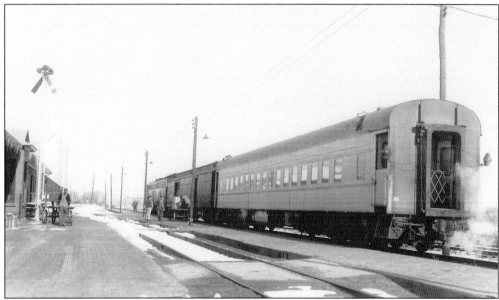

In March 1967, the CB&Q asked the Interstate Commerce Commission for discontinuance of passenger trains 42 and 43. (The trains were renumbered back to 41 and 42 in 1968). Area residents, local politicians, and labor unions put up a bitter legal fight to preserve the region's last vestige of public transportation. Now down to a two-car consist, 43 makes the usual transfer of express at Crawford on March 12, 1968. (A.J. Holck.)

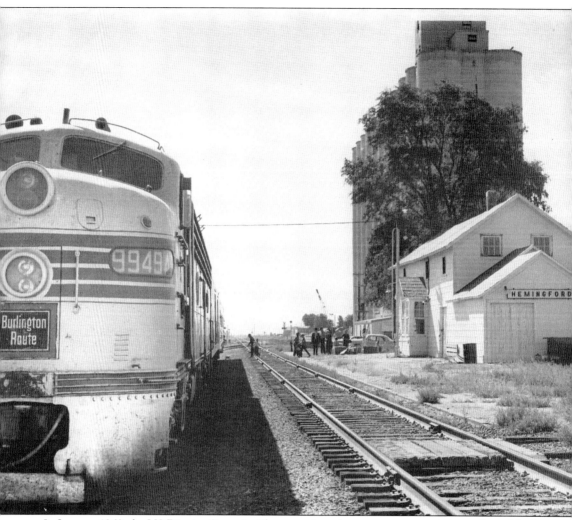

In January 1969, the US District Court in Cheyenne issued a temporary restraining order to block discontinuance of CB&Q trains 41 and 42. Then, in April, the ICC granted discontinuance, but court proceedings dragged on through the summer of 1969. On August 14, after the court ruled in favor of immediate discontinuance of the trains, CB&Q officials jumped at the chance. Train 42 was annulled at Billings, but 41 had already left Alliance when word came. It was stopped at Hemingford, Nebraska, the first town 19 miles up the line, where it is pictured here. Passengers and head-end traffic, after a delay of some hours, were bused on to their destinations. So great was the outcry over this cavalier interpretation of the court ruling that the matter went to the US Supreme Court, which then issued a 10-day order keeping the trains in operation. Trains 41 and 42 resumed operation until the end of that period. Ironically, almost nobody rode them for fear that another sudden ejection might take place. The trains then made their last runs on August 24, 1969. (The *Hemingford Ledger*, J.J. Reisdorff collection.)

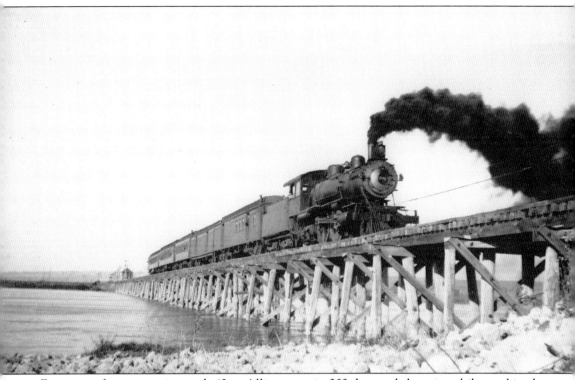

For years, after connecting with 43 at Alliance, train 303 departed that city while combined with train 31. At Bridgeport, Nebraska, the trains separated, with 303 continuing south for a late-afternoon arrival in Denver, while 31 backtracked to Northport, Nebraska, then headed west to Guernsey and Casper. Here, Denver-Alliance train 302, with vintage equipment pulled by a P2-class Atlantic, crosses the North Platte River at Northport in the early 1900s. A three-car train powered by a 4-6-2 was a typical consist for this line in the wake of the 1929 financial crash and the subsequent Great Depression. (J.L. Ehernberger collection.)

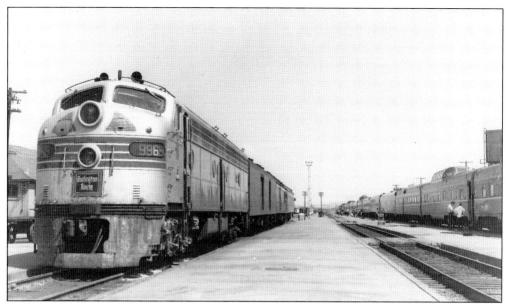

CB&Q train 30, powered by E8 No. 9965, was at Billings, Montana, on August 14, 1967. An eastbound Northern Pacific streamliner occupied an adjacent track. The northern roads of the James J. Hill empire carried the bulk of westbound passenger traffic from the Chicago region. Train 30, with its three-car consist, was scheduled to arrive in Denver at 7:35 a.m. the following morning after a 667-mile trip. (J.L. Ehernberger photograph.)

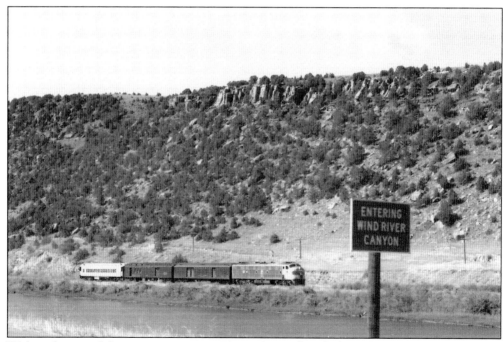

With its then-usual three-car consist, train 29 is at the north end of Wind River Canyon, Wyoming, on August 28, 1967. Trains 29 and 30 came off less than a week after this photograph was taken. (J.L. Ehernberger photograph.)

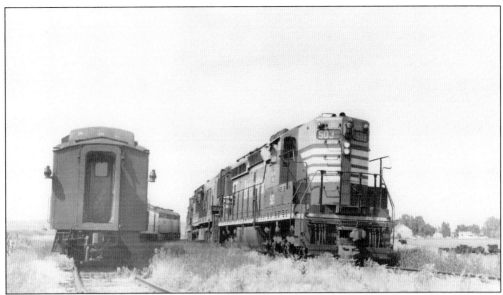

Billings-bound train 29 was "in the hole" for Casper-bound freight extra 503 while on Northern Pacific tracks at Silesia, Montana, 10 miles south of Laurel, on June 26, 1967. Now down to a baggage, railway post office, and chair car, trains 29 and 30 had carried a Pullman into the 1960s. (J.L. Ehernberger photograph.)

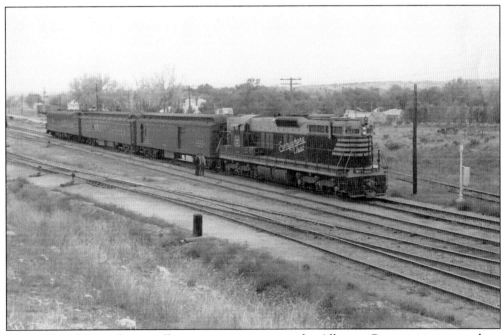

Trains 31 and 32 made virtually every station stop on the Alliance-Casper assignment along the North Platte River line. Train 31, with SD9 No. 345, waits at the west end of the Guernsey, Wyoming, yard in October 1963 for the arrival of two sections of freight train 78. Its regular two-car consist had been increased by the addition of office car 99 to accommodate a CB&Q general manager. (J.C. Seacrest, Corbin/Wagner collection.)

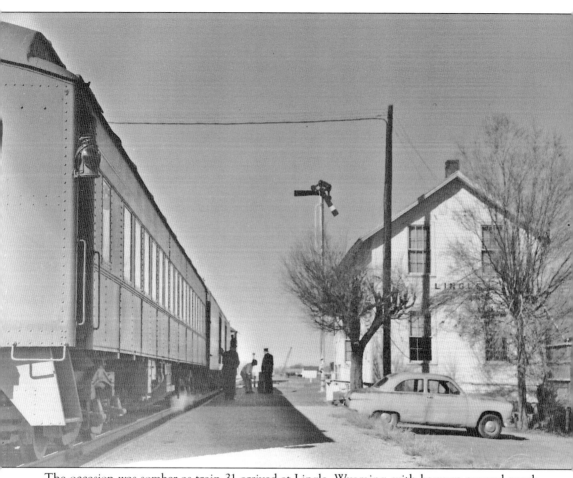
The occasion was somber as train 31 arrived at Lingle, Wyoming, with baggage car and coach on February 25, 1966. This train, with SD9 No. 350, was three days away from this assignment being annulled. Loss of the mail contract resulted in the dropping of trains 31 and 32. But, until the very end, head-end traffic had to be trans-loaded as usual. (J.L. Ehernberger photograph.)

Five

FREIGHT TRAIN SERVICE

The Chicago, Burlington & Quincy, as a stepchild to both the Great Northern and Northern Pacific, would ultimately have a traffic history comprised largely of hauling "leftover" through freight from Laurel Yard in Montana to Kansas City, while the Northern Pacific enjoyed the "gravy" by hauling eastbound priority traffic to the Twin Cities. The Burlington found itself frequently dragging trains of empties, from Kansas City back to Laurel, that had not necessarily moved over its rails as loads. Despite its secondary status, the Alliance Division did its job to expedite traffic. Lumber, perishable fruit, and other commodities moved over the line, plus, of course, coal, a major part of the traffic picture in the past as today. The Wyoming oil boom filled countless black tank cars over the decades. These "oilers" operated into the early 1950s and have returned in the second decade of the 21st century.

Ranching was a vital part of the region's economy; during the fall, the Burlington went all-out to give ranchers and sale barns the best service possible. Montana stations would load 30 cars of livestock, pile a half-dozen cowboys into a drover car, and rush them to Laurel. There, the Q would expedite this stock special so as to make Omaha within the 36-hour confinement law for feed and water. This traffic eventually was lost to trucks, but even as late as 1957, the CB&Q advertised special train service available to stock shippers. The final livestock movements came in the early 1970s.

Construction of irrigation canals in the North Platte Valley during the early 1900s encouraged sugar beet production. The Great Western Sugar Company eventually became the largest processor in the region, with plants at Gering, Bayard, Mitchell, Minatare, and Scottsbluff. Beets were also produced in the Hardin, Montana, area. Beet dumps were located at many stations, and several short spurs extended north in the Minatare and Scottsbluff areas. In time, these spurs were abandoned as beets were trucked to refineries and industry upheavals left Nebraska with one factory, at Scottsbluff, operated by successor Western Sugar Cooperative.

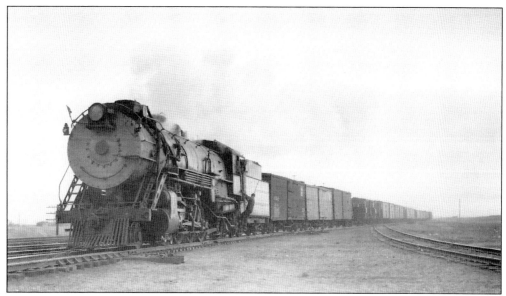

With a vintage consist that included a number of refrigerator cars, a 30-car westbound freight enters the Alliance yard on January 22, 1933. The head-end brakeman is poised on No. 5264's cab steps in order to drop off and align an approaching switch. The O2 Mikados were standard fare on the Alliance Division for freight service. (Otto Perry, Hol Wagner collection.)

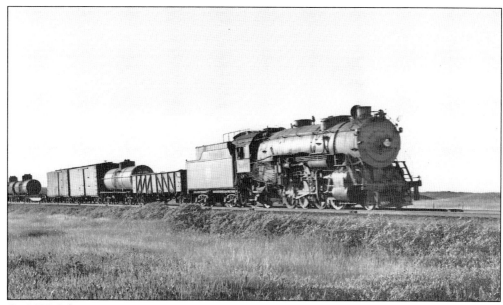

O4 USRA heavy 2-8-2 No. 5502 was eastbound near Anselmo, Nebraska, while operating Alliance-Lincoln with an extra freight on July 19, 1950. These oil-burning Mikados were assigned to Alliance from 1950 to 1955, just prior to the complete transition of freight service to diesels. (R.W. Buhrmaster, R.C. Kistler collection.)

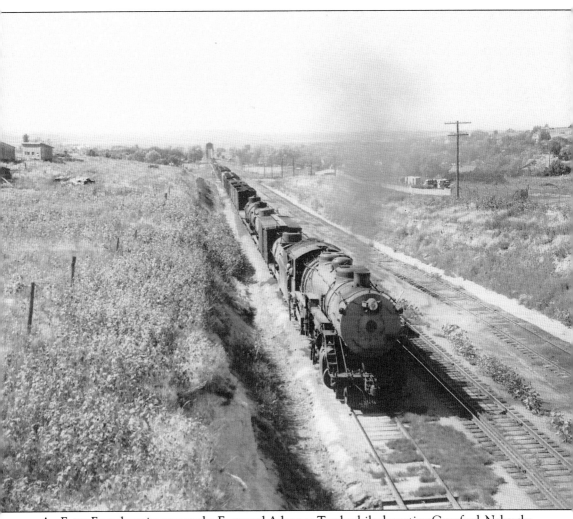

An Extra East chugs its way up the Eastward Advance Track while departing Crawford, Nebraska, on July 28, 1948. M2A locomotive No. 6152 repeated this scene countless times during its stay at Alliance from 1948 to 1950. In the distance is Crawford's coal tower and elevated ramp. (J.C. Hardy, J.L. Ehernberger collection.)

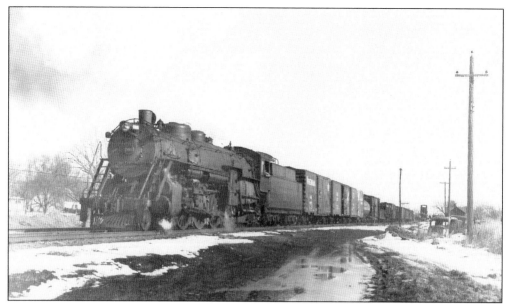

B1A No. 7019 leaves Broken Bow, Nebraska, with a westbound local freight on January 9, 1953. These trains were all-important to towns along the Ravenna-Alliance route, since they hauled grain, livestock, sugar beets, and goods and materials ordered by area business firms. The 7019 was one of three CB&Q Mountain types converted to oil that were assigned to Alliance from 1946 to 1954. (F.G. Gschwind, J.L. Ehernberger collection.)

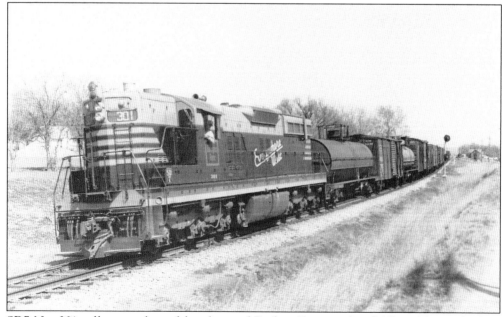

SD7 No. 301 rolls a westbound local out of Broken Bow on April 25, 1955. Locals then operated Ravenna-Seneca-Alliance-Edgemont, a practice that began in steam days and continued into the diesel era. These runs were often triweekly assignments. (F.G. Gschwind, J.L. Ehernberger collection.)

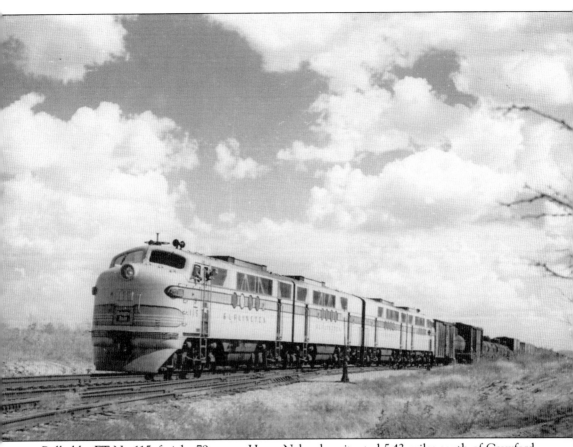

Pulled by FT No 115, freight 79 passes Horn, Nebraska, situated 5.43 miles south of Crawford, Nebraska, on August 15, 1947. Trains 79 and 80 moved a variety of goods along the Billings-Lincoln route. Judging by the position of the sun in this photograph, train 79 was on time, as it was scheduled to pass through Horn midday en route to Edgemont. The crew no doubt gave the photographer, a fellow "rail," a friendly wave as they rolled by. (J.C. Hardy, J.L. Ehernberger collection.)

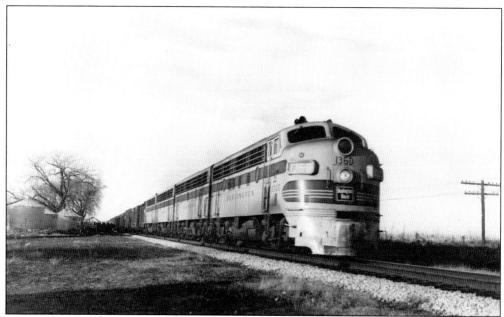

CB&Q 136D leads an eastbound freight through Merna, Nebraska, on December 3, 1961. The Ravenna subdivision was ladened with freight headed for Lincoln's hump yard, where it could be sorted and redirected toward either Kansas City or Chicago. The F units of EMD helped railroads like the Burlington "streamline" their freight service at a lower cost compared to using steam. (F.G. Gschwind, J.L. Ehernberger collection.)

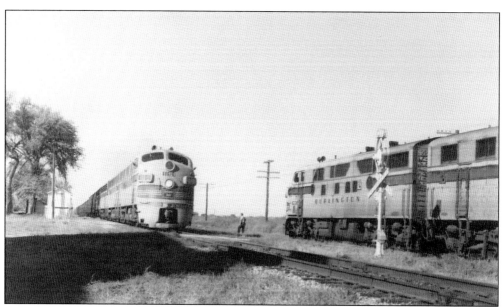

A meet of CB&Q freights at Merna, Nebraska, on October 13, 1964, finds the engineer of Extra 118-D East waving to the photographer. Meanwhile, the fireman waves to the trackside crew member of Extra 122-D West (train 75). The lead units of both trains could handle about 7,000 tons for Ravenna-Alliance, and about 8,200 tons eastbound. (F.G. Gschwind, J.L. Ehernberger collection.)

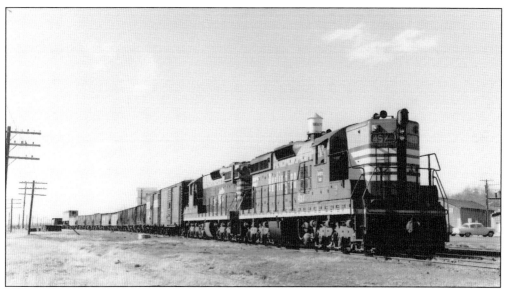

Extra 457 passes through Bridgeport, Nebraska, on April 16, 1967. Traffic levels on the one-time Sterling Division were minuscule compared with the flow of coal traffic today. (J.L. Ehernberger photograph.)

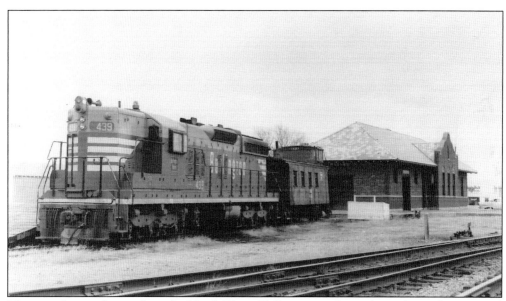

The sugar beet industry along the North Platte Valley required a road-switcher to be stationed at Bayard, Nebraska. Awaiting another call to service, SD9 439 and caboose 14383 are on the depot house spur on December 20, 1969. The Bayard depot was erected in 1928. (J.L. Ehernberger photograph.)

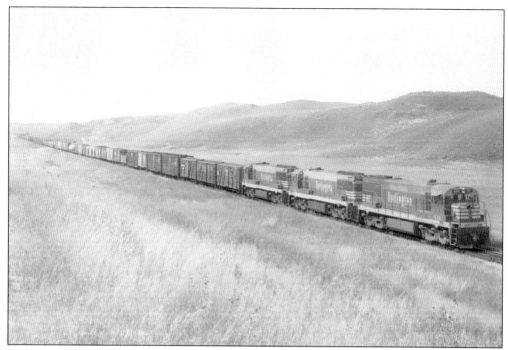

In a typical Sandhills scene west of Mullen, Nebraska, Burlington U28C No. 566, plus U25C Nos. 558 and 555, move a long freight through west central Nebraska on September 1, 1967. With Nebraska Highway 2 paralleling the Ravenna-Alliance main line most of the way, observing and photographing rail action on the route was fairly easy, even in CB&Q times. (Corbin/Wagner collection.)

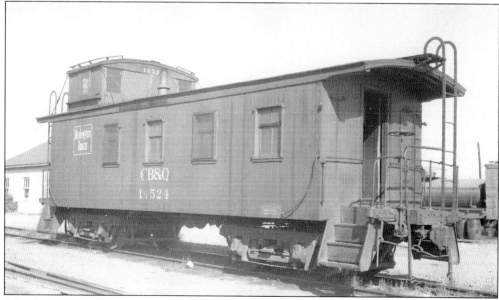

CB&Q caboose No. 14524 is seen at Casper, Wyoming, in August 1961. Built at the Aurora, Illinois, shops in October 1868, this trusty "hack" had no doubt by then traveled several million miles in freight service on the Burlington. But, 25 years later, cabooses would disappear as flashing rear-end detectors (FRED) were applied to freight trains. (A.J. Holck.)

Six

MOTIVE POWER

Due to the diversity of its terrain, the roster of motive power once assigned to the Alliance Division was the most varied of any Burlington Railroad division. The division used everything from narrow-gauge steam to electric trolley cars in the Black Hills, to large 2-6-6-2 type Mallets, used both in the Hills and on grades near Crawford and Bridgeport in Nebraska. Alliance also supplied the Sterling Division with much of its power. Prior to creation of the Casper Division, the Sheridan Division in 1914 maintained a fleet of 111 steam locomotives. In 1920, Casper had 66 locomotives and Sheridan 77.

In 1912, a National Parks Commission restriction required locomotives used in the Black Hills to burn oil to reduce fire danger. Meanwhile, the oil-rich Casper area made it economical for engines to burn oil at that point, while Sheridan had a ready supply of coal. By 1925, Casper had oil burners in every class from K10 to O4. Alliance and Sterling power, especially all 2-6-2s, were retrofitted as oil burners for service in required areas.

In March 1932, the Burlington took delivery of a 400-horsepower Whitcomb gas-electric switch engine, No. 9120. Its testing included a trip with the Spearfish, South Dakota, branch train on May 6–7, 1932. The first diesels assigned to Alliance were EMD NW2s Nos. 9216 and 9218, both appearing on the September 1, 1942, assignment sheet. In 1950, Alco S2 switchers were used in Alliance, where they stayed until being transferred to Denver in June 1958. The first road freight diesels, "grayback" FTs, made their debut in July 1944, heralding the start of system power pools. Diesels began appearing on passenger trains 42 and 43 in November 1947.

By 1950, Casper had its first assigned diesels: NW2 No. 9229 and six 9400 series NW2s. Sheridan had NW2 No. 9236. Within several years, diesels assumed all Casper and Sheridan operations, with Sterling soon to follow. The Burlington assigned GP7s Nos. 201 and 202 as the first road switchers at Alliance in October 1951. Next to arrive in 1954 were GP9s, while SD7 and SD9 units also came then in force. The last year for steam at Alliance was 1955, with only four engines remaining. SD9s became the dominant freight power until new GE U25Bs began arriving in October 1964. Retired steam locomotives were donated by the Burlington to the towns of Alliance, Douglas, and Sheridan as reminders of the service once given by the "iron horse" in developing the region.

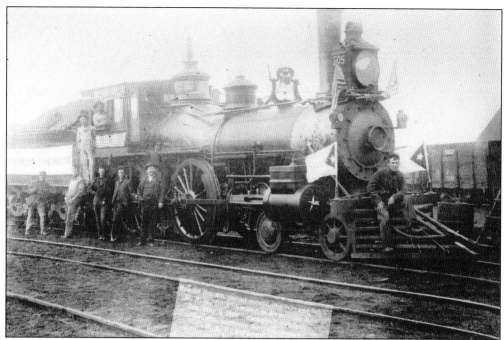

B&MR No. 205, an A1 4-4-0, had arrived in Newcastle, Wyoming, from Sheridan while hauling Wyoming National Guard companies O and G on May 2, 1898. Guard colors are mounted on the pilot beam, US flag detailing adorns the headlight and cab sides, and the tender is emblazoned with a "Remember the Maine" banner. The unexplained explosion and sinking of the US battleship *Maine* in Havana harbor on February 15, 1898, led to the Spanish-American War and the activation of National Guard troops. (Corbin/Wagner collection.)

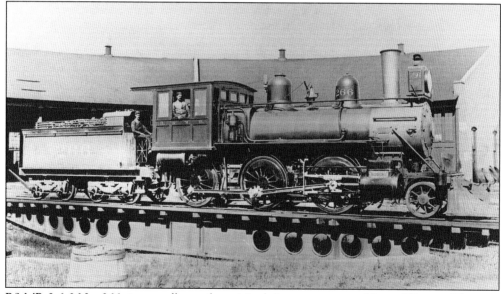

B&MR 2-6-0 No. 266 sits proudly on the original Armstrong turntable at Alliance. The trim H-class Moguls intended for general service were capable of moving light-passenger assignments at speed. In 1904, H1 Moguls were given a tonnage rating of 1,000 tons for Ravenna-Alliance in slow freight service and 550 tons on westbound fast freights. (Alliance Knight Museum.)

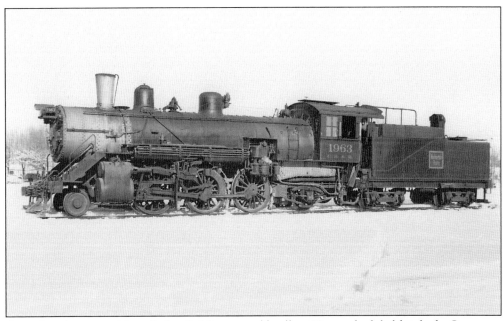

A good engine crew with an R-class 2-6-2 type could pull an 80-car scheduled freight for Guernsey-Northport without a helper. A fireman had his true test on hand-fired steamers north of Northport, Nebraska, over Angora Hill even with a helper. Oil burners were always welcome. Seen here waiting assignment at Sterling, Colorado, on November 20, 1953, is No. 1963. (C.L. Ulrich, R.C. Kistler collection.)

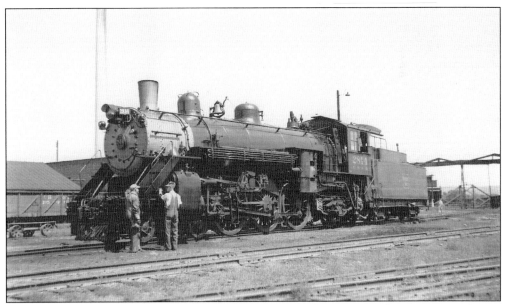

Here, two Casper, Wyoming, roundhouse employees attend to S1A Pacific No. 2814 in August 1938. Assigned to passenger service out of Casper, the well-maintained 4-6-2 was transferred there from McCook, Nebraska, in 1925. A 1906 Baldwin Locomotive Works product, it produced 32,770 pounds tractive effort. (Corbin/Wagner collection.)

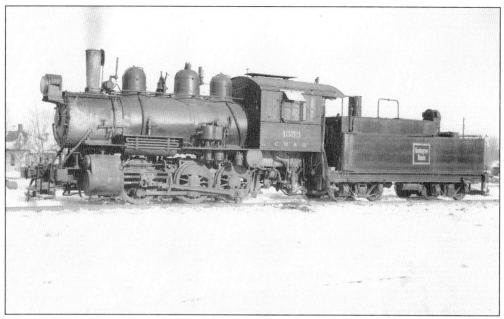

After being reassigned in 1951 from the Alliance Division to the Casper Division, G3 class 0-6-0 No. 1553 was again transferred in 1953. This time, it was sent to Sterling, Colorado, to spend about a year there. Pictured at Sterling on November 21, 1953, the little Baldwin was far from its former switching assignment at Deadwood, South Dakota. (C.L. Ulrich, R.C. Kistler collection.)

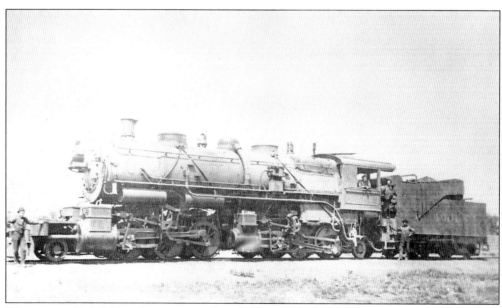

T1 compound 2-6-6-2 No. 4001 was new from Baldwin and assigned to helper service at Crawford, Nebraska, when pictured there in 1908. It had 70,000 pounds tractive effort, 56-inch drivers, and a total engine weight of 354,500 pounds. It took two firemen shoveling coal to satisfy the ferocious appetite of this beast. It was scrapped in 1927. (Corbin/Wagner collection.)

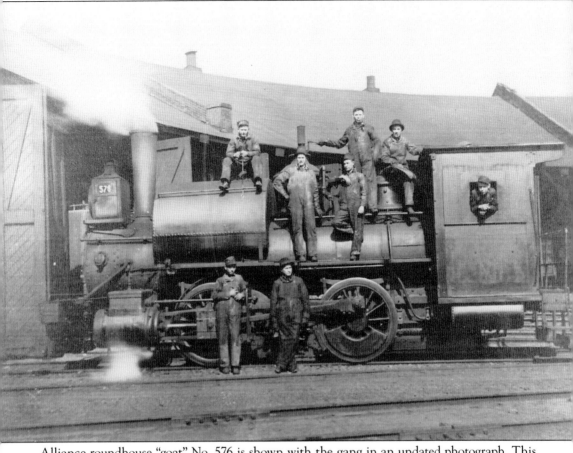

Alliance roundhouse "goat" No. 576 is shown with the gang in an undated photograph. This diminutive 0-4-0T (saddle tank) engine handled larger engines in and out of the facility. The 576 was originally built at West Burlington Shops in 1887. Its last year at Alliance was 1915. The last use of steam as a shop switcher at Alliance was in 1954. (Alliance Knight Museum.)

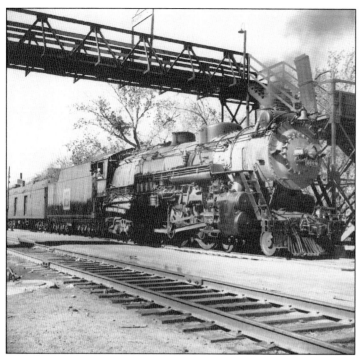

Burlington's S4 and S4A class 4-6-4 Hudsons were the most handsome locomotives to burnish CB&Q rails. S4A No. 4001 was built new at West Burlington Shops in 1938, with a streamlined shroud applied to serve as standby power for the Zephyr streamliners. The shroud was removed in early 1942. Here, No. 4000 shows off a fresh coat of paint while at Alliance with train 44 on October 16, 1947. (J.C. Hardy, J.L. Ehernberger collection.)

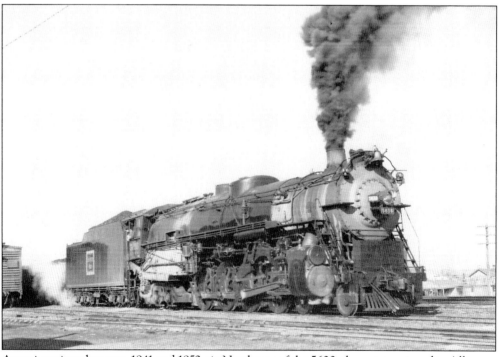

At various times between 1941 and 1952, six Northerns of the 5600-class were assigned to Alliance. O5A No. 5616, photographed at Alliance on February 16, 1947, carried 27 tons of coal and 18,000 gallons of water, produced 67,500 pounds of tractive force, and stood 16 feet, 2 inches from rail to the top of its stack. These were impressive statistics for an engine equally adapted to both heavy-passenger and freight service. (J.C. Hardy, J.L. Ehernberger collection.)

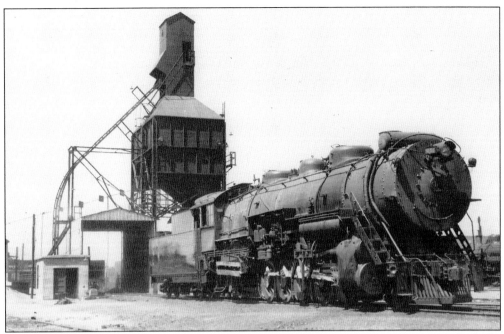

The pride and joy of Alliance Division steam freight power were the M2A 2-10-2s, into which the CB&Q incorporated all the latest mechanical innovations of the era. These included elongated water tanks. Engine No. 6156 sits on the Alliance coal chute track, its ash pan open, awaiting a fire cleaning in the summer of 1947. (Corbin/Wagner collection.)

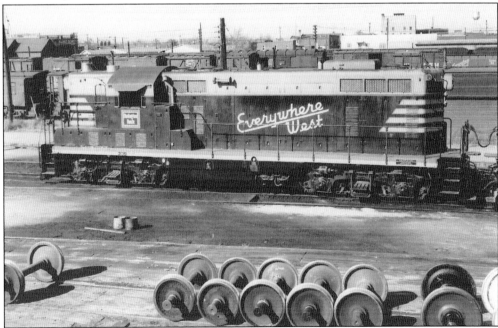

Prior to the arrival of the SD9 class that would end regular steam operations, three GP7 diesels worked out of Alliance. GP7 No. 239 is seen at Alliance on September 22, 1952. The units were versatile, but fell short on power efficiency for Deadwood branch and Crawford Hill assignments. (J.C. Hardy, J.L. Ehernberger collection.)

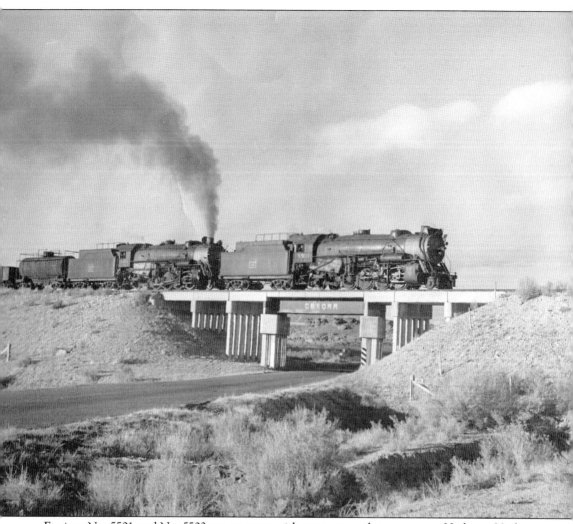

Engines No. 5501 and No. 5503 are en route with tonnage as they cross over Highway 20 about three miles from Bonneville, Wyoming, around 1950. Freights 75 and 76 were then in daily service for Casper-Billings. These impressive-looking O4 class 2-8-2s were the last steam engines assigned to freight service on the Casper Division, with several serving as the last regularly assigned steam on the Burlington's western divisions. (C.G. Dewey, Hol Wagner collection.)

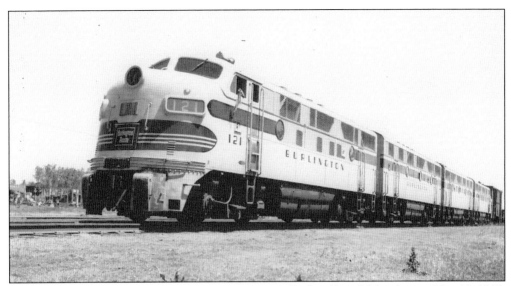

Built in late 1947, the four-unit F3 No. 121 is seen at Broken Bow, Nebraska, on May 16, 1948. A number of these locomotives, by late 1948, were assigned to mainline freight service across Nebraska, resulting in the eventual retirement of Mikado and Mountain-type steam locomotives. (A.J. Holck.)

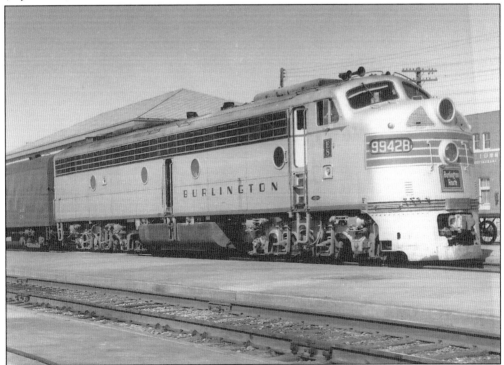

CB&Q E8 No. 9942B is shown in passenger service at Billings, Montana, on August 1, 1963. E8 units with 2,250 horsepower could be operated as a single unit for shorter passenger trains, or in multiple and with other models to handle heavier assignments, such as the Zephyrs. E8s saw regular service during the last years of passenger service on the Lincoln-Billings line. (W.F. Rapp, R.C. Kistler collection.)

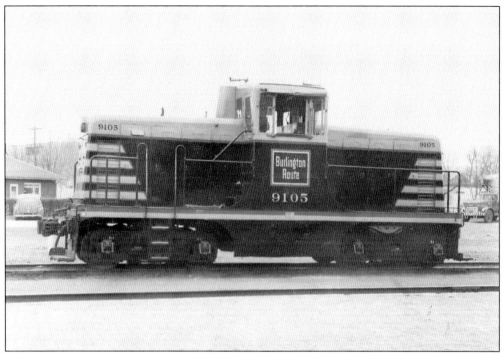

General Electric 44-ton switcher No. 9105, one of five on the CB&Q, was built in 1941. It replaced an 0-6-0 steam engine at Scottsbluff, Nebraska, where it is pictured on April 15, 1954. However, this assignment proved too much for the little center cab, which had only 360 horsepower. It was replaced by a heavier unit. (J.C. Hardy, J.L. Ehernberger collection.)

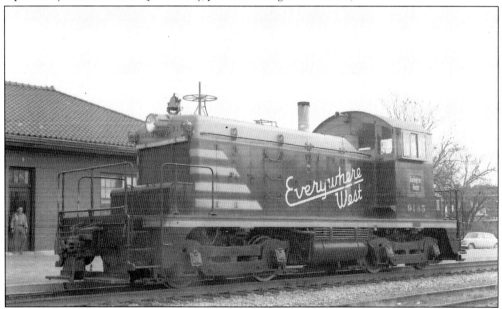

SW1 No. 9145 waits for a crew who will use it for their next switch assignment at Scottsbluff, Nebraska, on October 24, 1968. The 600-horsepower EMD product produced 50,000 pounds of tractive effort. Built in May 1940, No. 9145 became Burlington Northern No. 90 in 1970 and was then assigned to Lincoln Division duties. (A.J. Wolff.)

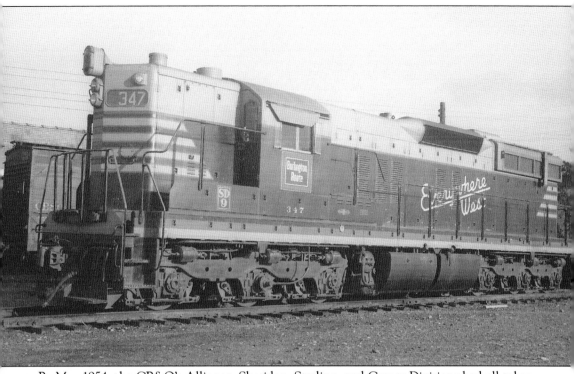

By May 1954, the CB&Q's Alliance, Sheridan, Sterling, and Casper Divisions had all taken delivery of EMD-built SD7 and SD9 units. A consequence of this was a long list of condemned steam power on the Burlington's system assignment sheet. Diesel-electrics such as SD9 No. 347, pictured here at Casper, Wyoming, on October 1, 1961, would be remembered for having taken over traffic duties not already held by other diesel power. (A.J. Holck.)

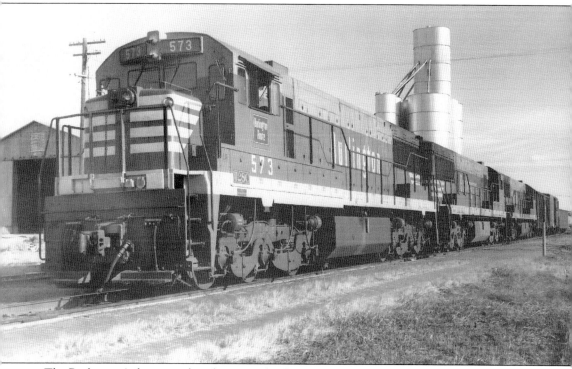

The Burlington's departure from buying only Electro Motive road engines first occurred in 1964, when it ordered six units, each with 2,500 horsepower, from General Electric. A year later, a dozen 2,500-horsepower U25C units were acquired. In 1966, twenty U28Bs (2,800 horsepower) and sixteen U28Cs were ordered. These units soon appeared on Alliance Division freight trains. Pictured at Broken Bow, Nebraska, on December 19, 1966, this mainline freight was headed by three "U-boats." For a time, these units were the primary power source for Ravenna-Alliance freight service. (F.G. Gschwind, J.L. Ehernberger collection.)

Seven
ALLIANCE RAIL FACILITIES AND DIVISION EVENTS

Like many railroad division point towns across the United States in the steam era, Alliance once maintained a number of now-vanished support structures for its motive power and passenger and freight service. As an example, a tour of Alliance rail facilities in the mid-1940s would begin at the passenger depot and division headquarters. A short distance west was the service building occupied by Railway Express Agency (REA) and car inspectors. About two blocks west of the REA building was the freight house. Meanwhile, across the street, northwest of the passenger depot, was the Alliance Hotel and Cafe.

Immediately south of the passenger depot was a 13-track freight yard where most switching was done from the west, since the cars would slowly roll east downhill. Directly east of the depot was a footbridge over the yard used by shop employees and engine men going to and from work. Near the south end of the footbridge, to the west, was the master mechanic's office building.

A short distance east of the master mechanic's office was the icehouse, capable of servicing seven ice-cooled refrigerator cars. South of the icehouse were "rip" tracks where cars were repaired. South of the rip tracks were the water tank, coal chute, and sand bins. South of these structures were the stockyards, which featured enough feed pens to handle an entire stock train.

A runaround track skirted the yard's south rim. Fanning out between the freight yard and runaround track was the roundhouse. On its north end were five short stalls originally constructed by the Burlington & Missouri River. On its northwest corner was a two-stall back shop with two tracks extending from inside the roundhouse. West of the roundhouse was the powerhouse, which provided steam for stationary engines. Nearby was the storehouse, containing an inventory of spare parts for locomotives, cars, buildings, and track. Adjacent to the storehouse was the roundhouse facility's main water standpipe, with diesel-fuel tanks situated below it. West of the standpipe was a water-treatment plant where soda ash was added to keep engine boilers from foaming. Northwest of the plant was the oil house, where lubricants were kept.

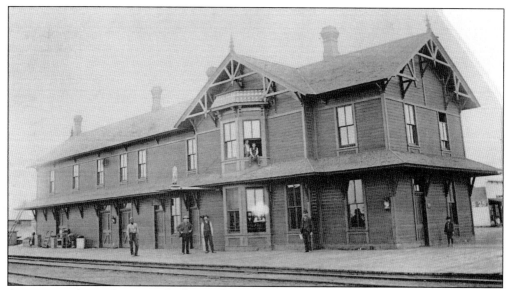

A two-story frame depot was built at Alliance in 1888 to replace the town's original station building. The design was similar to other Burlington & Missouri River division point station buildings. Pictured here around 1895, the depot by 1905 had a second bay window added to the second story for the division superintendent's office. While masterpieces of masonry, one of its four chimneys caused the structure to catch fire and burn on November 24, 1906. It was replaced on the same site by a larger brick structure. (Alliance Knight Museum.)

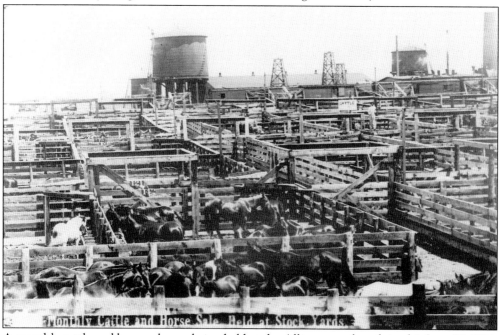

A monthly cattle and horse sale was being held at the Alliance stockyards in this June 25, 1914, photograph. Pens near the track were utilized as rest stops for cattle shipped from Montana and Wyoming to Omaha. From the 1920s through the 1960s, full trainloads of cattle were common in the fall. By the time the stock pens here were dismantled in 1975, railroads like the Burlington had lost their livestock business to trucks. (Hol Wagner collection.)

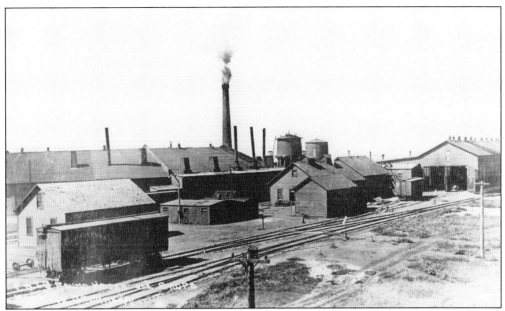

The CB&Q roundhouse and shops at Alliance are seen here around 1910, looking west from a point near the master mechanic's office. Visible is the two-stall back shop that extended into the north end of the roundhouse. The latter was located north of the turntable. (Alliance Knight Museum.)

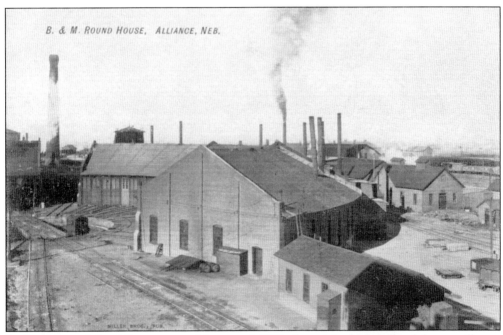

Looking toward the Alliance turntable around 1900, the original 15 stalls of the roundhouse built by the Burlington & Missouri River Railroad are visible at right. These stalls, used in the CB&Q period for smaller engines, were removed around 1951. Later, 12 larger stalls were added to the south side of this structure. (Hol Wagner collection.)

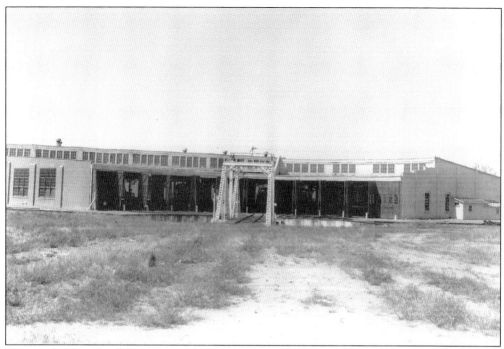

The south 12 stalls of the Alliance roundhouse remained as of June 28, 1968. During the last years of CB&Q steam, they had housed larger power, such as the M2A 2-10-2s. This structure was removed in 1980 as part of BN's rearrangement of its Alliance yard facilities, with the turntable retained for additional service. (Corbin/Wagner collection.)

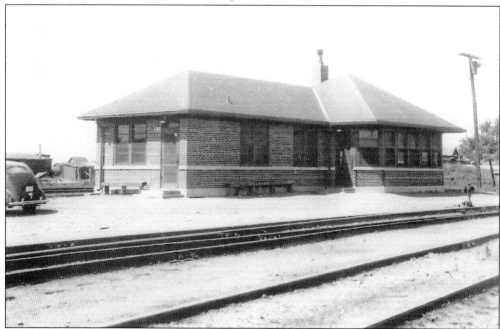

The old Alliance yard office was located about three blocks west of the depot, on the yard's south side. Seen here on February 5, 1950, the brick structure was later used as the yardmen's locker room after yard office duties were moved into the depot. (J.C. Hardy, J.L. Ehernberger collection.)

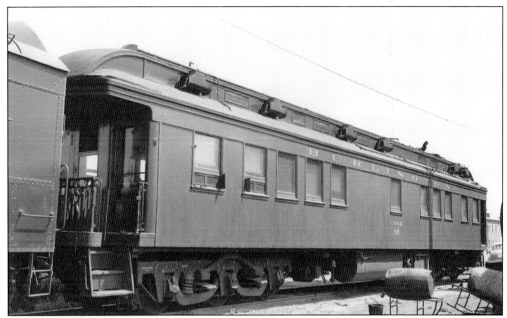

CB&Q office car 89 is at Alliance on July 20, 1950. Built by Pullman in 1892 as a chair car, it was converted at Plattsmouth, Nebraska, in 1897 to a B&MR office car for Lines West general manager George W. Holdrege. It became CB&Q office car 89 in 1904. Assigned to Alliance in the late 1930s as the division superintendent's office car, it held this assignment until retirement in December 1955. (R.W. Buhrmaster, R.C. Kistler collection.)

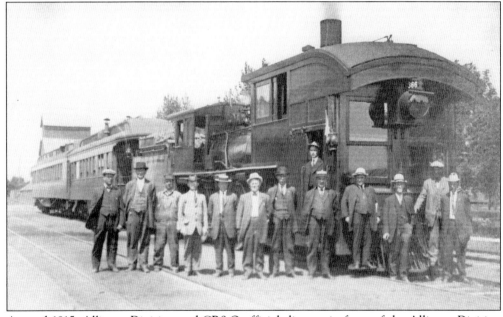

Around 1915, Alliance Division and CB&Q officials line up in front of the Alliance Division inspection engine, A2 No. 366. Built in 1878 as B&MR No. 24, the *Brownville*, the 4-4-0 was rebuilt by Havelock Shops in July 1897. It was converted to an inspection engine around 1912, and retired in 1928. While the 366 gave officials a better view of the company's roadbed, the office cars behind it certainly afforded the gentlemen more comfort. (J.L. Ehernberger collection.)

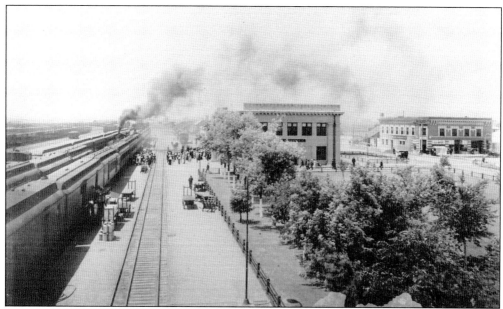

Train time at Alliance, around 1915, shows that train 44 from Billings has drawn a crowd of onlookers as well as passengers. Train 44 then included a coach, chair car, Pullman, and diner. To the right of the depot is the Alliance Hotel and Restaurant. Present was the 0-6-0 yard engine that worked the 13-track terminal. (Alliance Knight Museum.)

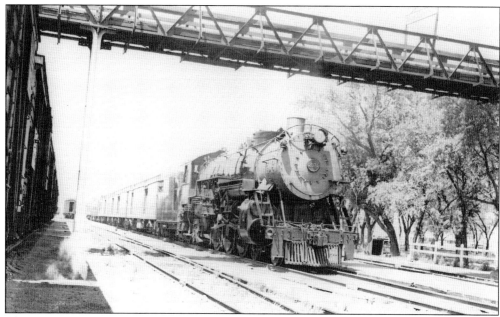

This scene was repeated daily as passenger trains stopped at the Alliance depot, their motive power pausing across from the tree-lined depot park. Framed by the overhead walkway, 4-6-2 No. 2967 was headed east with train 44 on April 26, 1946. The walkway carried workers to and from the roundhouse situated across from the depot. (A.W. Madison, Corbin/Wagner collection.)

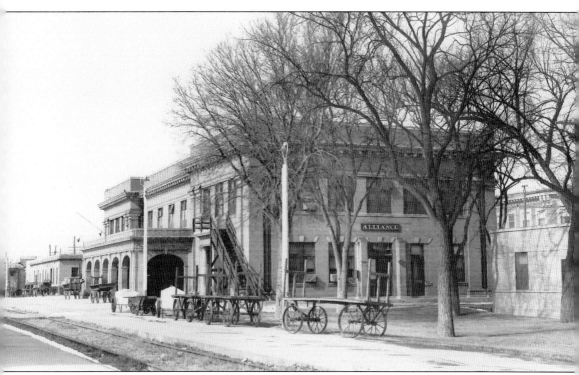

The 57-foot-by-145-foot Alliance passenger and division office building was constructed in 1907. Seen here on February 18, 1968, baggage trucks are positioned along the brick platform, while at right is a small building for CTC battery and equipment storage. At left is the service building; its east end was occupied by Railway Express and its west end by "car toad" mechanics. The spur track in front of the service building was usually occupied by a surplus railway post-office or baggage car. The depot housed 23 division superintendents over the years. When CTC was installed, the dispatcher's office was moved downstairs. Following the end of passenger service in 1969, the entire ground floor became the yard office. The yardmaster then had his lookout built atop the south trackside canopy. A new Alliance Division office building for officials and dispatchers was constructed in 1979 on the site of the service building and freight house. The depot was demolished on March 8, 1980. (J.L. Ehernberger photograph.)

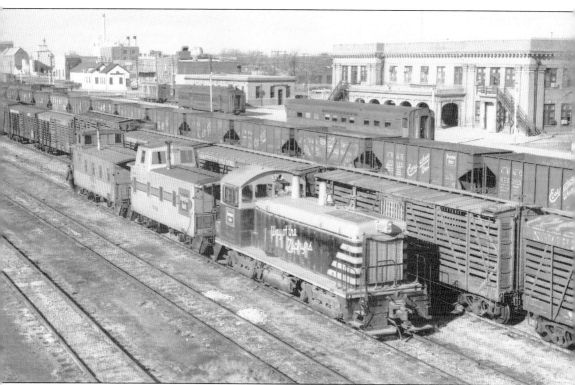

SW12 No. 9280 shoves two cabooses through the Alliance yard on November 12, 1968. To comply with a Colorado law requiring all cabooses in that state be fitted with electric lights, the Burlington repainted three NE10-class steel cabooses, so fitted with electric lights, in an orange scheme so they could easily be identified as such—as is the rear caboose in this photograph. These cabooses were primarily used on trains 71 and 72 operating between Alliance and Sterling. In front of the depot is Pullman No. 465, *Silver Tulip*. At left, an RPO car is spotted aside the service building, while beyond it is the freight house, equipped with a track and dock on either side. (A.J. Wolff.)

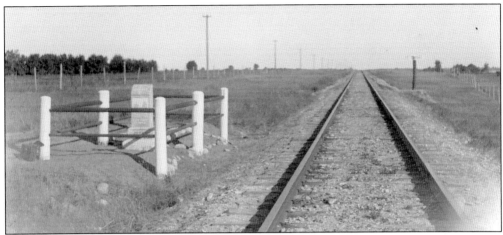

The grave of Rebecca Winters is one of a few marked along the historic Mormon Trail, used by members of The Church of Jesus Christ of Latter-day Saints in their westward trek to Utah. Winters had been one of some 6,000 LDS pioneers who died making the journey across the plains. On August 15, 1852, she succumbed to cholera while traveling with her family near Chimney Rock. Her grave on the trail was marked by an iron wagon tire with her name carved on it. When the railroad arrived 48 years later, the Burlington built a protective fence around the grave. In 1902, Rebecca's descendants from Utah erected a monument. (Nebraska State Historical Society.)

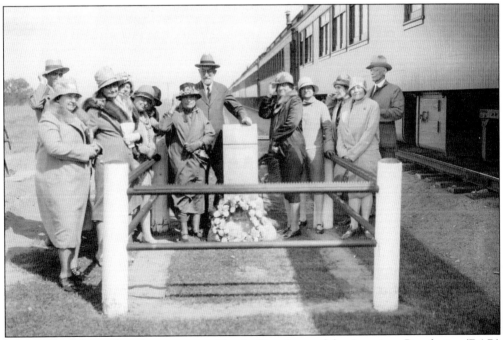

In 1929, an additional marker was erected by the Daughters of the American Revolution (DAR) at the Rebecca Winters gravesite. Here, a CB&Q train carrying DAR and Mormon officials pauses at the grave. However, due to an increasing number of coal trains passing the site, the BN in 1995 decided to relocate the grave for visitor safety. In September 1995, Winters's remains were exhumed and moved a short distance from the original location. In June 1996, hundreds of her descendants gathered for the dedication of the Rebecca Winters Memorial Park. (Nebraska State Historical Society.)

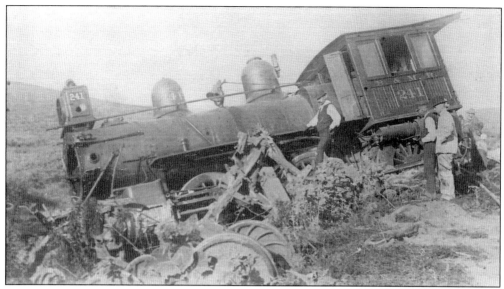

Several gentlemen look over the situation after B&MR 4-4-0 No. 241 had obviously jumped the track somewhere between Ravenna and Alliance around 1895. Unfortunately, information regarding this particular incident has not surfaced. No. 241, built by the Baldwin Locomotive Works in 1890, later became CB&Q No. 1026 when renumbered in January 1905. (Hol Wagner collection.)

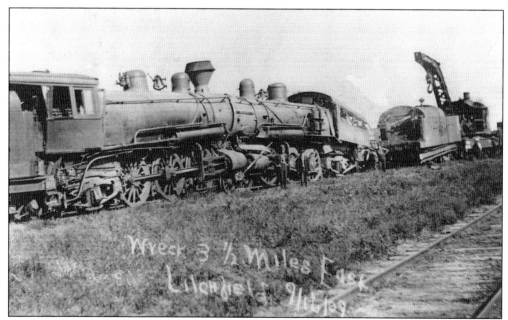

A head-on collision between freight train No. 45 and a livestock extra occurred two and a half miles west of Hazard, Nebraska, on September 16, 1909. The locomotives, both 2-6-2 types, with No. 2219 on the stock train, had telescoped upon impact. Both engine crews had jumped and suffered various injuries. About 300 sheep were killed on the stock train. It was determined that No. 45's crew had overlooked an order to pass the other train at Hazard. (J.L. Ehernberger collection.)

Among the dangers of the steam age were boiler explosions. A Burlington freight engine, 2-8-2 No. 5020, exploded near Provo, South Dakota, at 12:05 a.m. on February 15, 1913, killing the engineer, fireman, and head brakeman. The train did not derail, but the force of the explosion sent the boiler flying entirely beyond the right-of-way. This locomotive was returned to service. (Hol Wagner collection.)

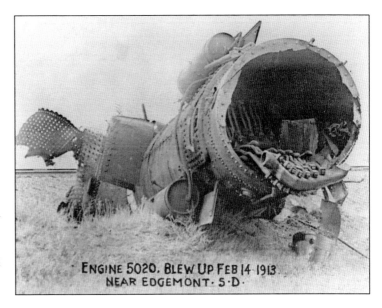

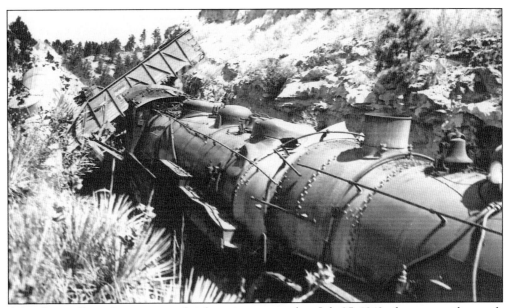

A head-on collision between two freight trains occurred on July 25, 1942, about two miles north of Belmont, Nebraska, resulting in three deaths and four severe injuries among the train crews. The Crawford operator failed to deliver an order changing the location of a meet. The trains collided in a cut near Belmont Tunnel with little advance visibility. Freight cars were spewed throughout the cut. (J.C. Hardy, J.L. Ehernberger collection.)

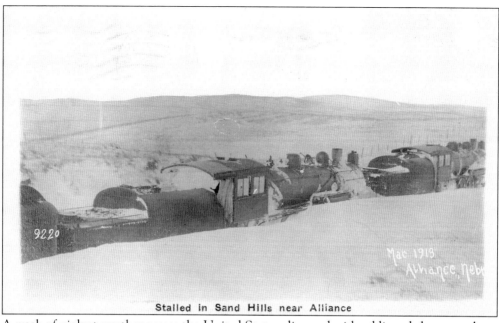

Stalled in Sand Hills near Alliance

A week of violent weather across the United States climaxed with a blizzard that roared out of the Colorado Rockies into northwestern Nebraska, hitting Alliance on the morning of March 13, 1913. A Burlington passenger train with S1 Pacifics Nos. 2807 and 2815 stalled in the drifting snow at Ellsworth, Nebraska, near Alliance. The train became buried, with snow filling the cabs of both engines, and near-zero temperatures turning the cars into blocks of ice. (Hol Wagner collection.)

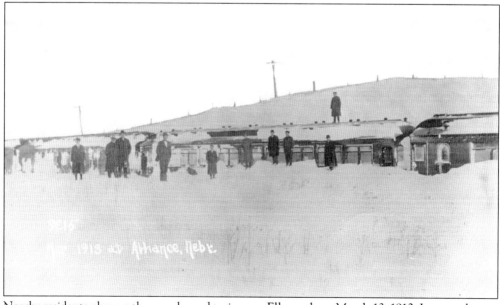

Nearby residents observe the snowbound train near Ellsworth on March 13, 1913. It was only part of a statewide tragedy resulting from freakish weather conditions. A massive loss of livestock was suffered by area ranchers. Meanwhile, a series of tornadoes in eastern Nebraska that afternoon and evening hit both small towns and the Omaha metropolitan area. The death toll around Omaha was 94, out of an overall total of 150 casualties. (Hol Wagner collection.)

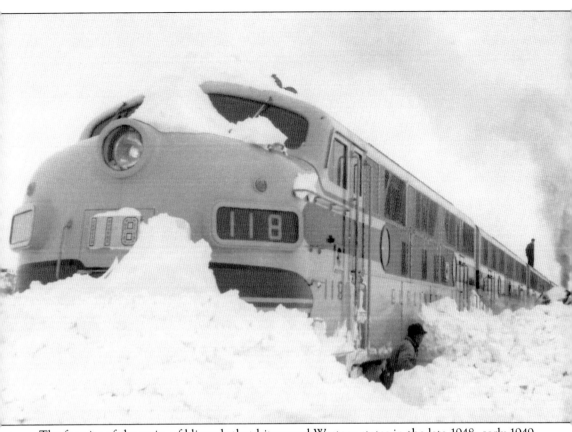

The ferocity of the series of blizzards that hit several Western states in the late 1948–early 1949 period stopped all forms of travel. On January 17, 1949, CB&Q F3 diesel No. 118 was stuck in a long cut north of Edgemont, South Dakota, at milepost 3 on the Deadwood line. Edgemont yard engine No. 5055 failed to budge it. So, a huskier M2A steam engine tried until its coupler broke. The only way out of the hard-packed snow was to dig by hand. Anyone who could grab a shovel was hired. (J.C. Hardy, J.L. Ehernberger collection.)

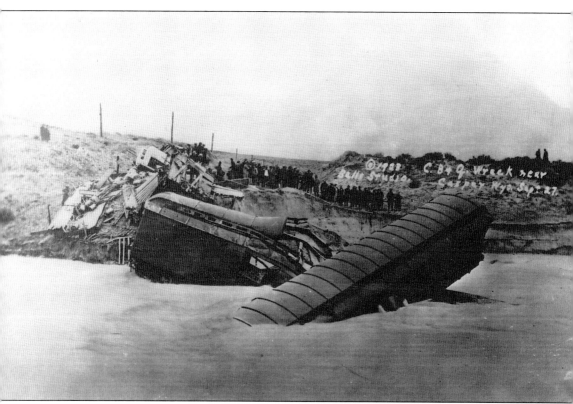

On September 27, 1923, a disastrous accident involving passenger train No. 30 eastbound from Casper, Wyoming, occurred as a result of high water on Cole Creek at Lockett, Wyoming, 14 miles east of Casper. A severe storm had destroyed a pile trestle at that point prior to the passage of No. 30. The engine plunged into the raging water, followed by a baggage car that shot over the locomotive onto the opposite bank, then a baggage/mail car, two coaches, and a Pullman, the latter becoming partially submerged. The greatest loss of life was in the coaches, which went under the swirling, mud-filled water. Here, an all-steel coach juts out of the streambed, and the baggage end of a baggage/mail car rests to the left. The shattered remains of a baggage car are on the far (east) bank. Spectators line both sides of the swollen stream. It was difficult to locate bodies even after the floodwaters receded. According to an accident investigation report, the deaths of seventeen passengers and four employees were recorded, with seven passengers and three employees listed as missing. (A.J. Holck collection.)

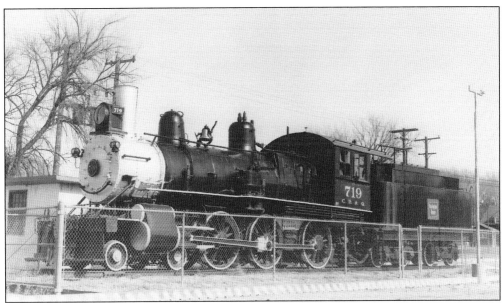

There were always several 4-6-0s assigned to Alliance for duty, either in the Black Hills or on the light-railed branch line between Sterling and Cheyenne. One of them, No. 719, following its last assignment at McCook, Nebraska, was hauled to Lincoln in 1958. From there, it was transported to Alliance in 1962 and given to the town for display. After 18 years at its original location, where it is depicted here in February 1968, No. 719 was taken to the Alliance BN shops in 1980 and cosmetically restored. In 1982, it was moved to its current display site along Box Butte Avenue. Other steam locomotives on display in the former Alliance Division region are two 4-8-4s, No. 5631 at Sheridan, Wyoming, and No. 5633 at Douglas, Wyoming. (J.L. Ehernberger photograph.)

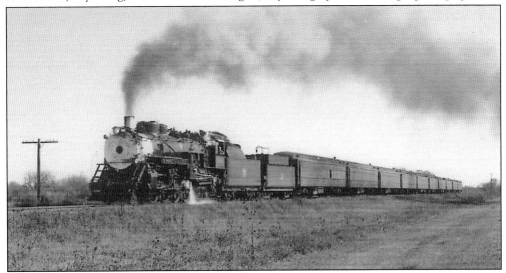

The last active CB&Q steam on Alliance Division trackage occurred when the CB&Q ran "Steam Choo-Choo" specials with Mikado No. 4960. The 2-8-2 went to Casper in October 1963 for the 50th anniversary of CB&Q service to that town. On October 28 that year, it made a Broken Bow–Ravenna round-trip for the kids. Here, the engine struts with a 10-car train west of Ravenna, Nebraska. Retired by the Burlington in 1966, the engine was eventually acquired for tourist service on the Grand Canyon Railway in Arizona. (F.G. Gschwind, J.L. Ehernberger collection.)

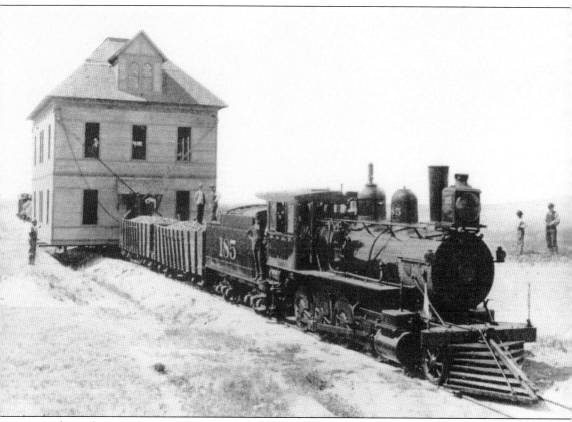

Perhaps the most famous photograph in Alliance-area railroad history is this view of the Box Butte County Courthouse being moved by train from Hemingford, Nebraska, to Alliance in July 1899. This was the result of an election that relocated the county seat to Alliance. B&MR general manager G.W. Holdrege enlisted the railroad's help for this daring job. With the use of reinforced flatcars, the two-story frame building was moved 19 miles in 21 hours. B&MR 2-8-0 No. 185, built by the Baldwin Locomotive Works in 1888, was freshly painted for this exploit. (J.L. Ehernberger collection.)

Eight
The Burlington Northern Era

An assimilation of the James J. Hill Lines into one large rail system had been proposed and attempted for many years. The longstanding goal of unifying the Chicago, Burlington & Quincy with the Great Northern, Northern Pacific, and the Spokane, Portland & Seattle railroads finally took place on March 2, 1970, creating Burlington Northern Inc. Almost concurrent with the merger was the tremendous growth in low-sulfur coal traffic. During the five-year period of 1978–1982, BN invested more than $1 billion in the Alliance Division physical plant to meet traffic demands. This included construction of the longest US rail line since 1931, the 116-mile Orin Line to tap Wyoming's Powder River Basin, completed on November 6, 1979. A buildup of this magnitude in such a short time span is rare by industry standards. The region was transformed from a division that handled a handful of trains a day in the early 1970s to one handling more than 150 daily.

The impact on Alliance was dramatic. The workforce jumped from a scant 150 in the early 1970s to more than 2,000 by 1980. The city's population grew from 7,000 to 10,000 in a decade. A new main shop facility that went into limited operation on October 23, 1978, incorporated five separate areas, the largest designed for diesel locomotive repair. The materials department filled a two-story building. Also in 1978, an additional 30,000 feet of Alliance yard track was placed in service, with 13-year-old yard tracks improved, and 12 new tracks built alongside the 3rd Subdivision Sterling main in order to handle coal trains. A new yard office, plus a tower from which the yardmaster could view both yards, went into service on January 23, 1979. Also added was a new one-story division office building, costing $1.3 million. Placed in service in early 1980 was the new Alliance South Yard to support the existing, but completely remodeled, North Yard.

At its peak, Alliance boasted 33 train dispatchers handling 1,042 miles of Alliance Division main and branch lines. However, effective October 20, 1988, the Alliance Division was abolished. Its territory was split up between the Nebraska Division and a newly formed Denver Division. But by January 1, 1993, the Alliance Division had been reestablished, with the Powder River Division, based in Gillette, Wyoming, covering territory west of Edgemont. However, the new incarnation of the Alliance Division would be short-lived, as it disappeared once again with the start of the BNSF era three years later.

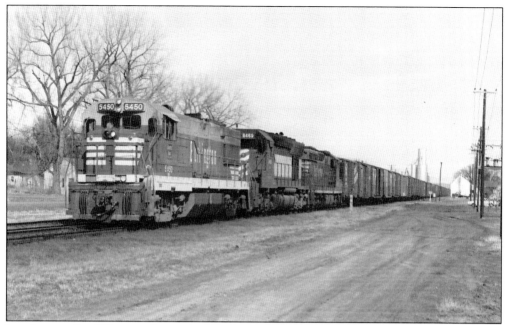

Iron horses of a different color marked Burlington Northern's early years. On March 30, 1971, a westbound freight leaves Broken Bow, Nebraska. It has three ex-CB&Q units as power: U28B No. 5450 in red-white, SD45 No. 6469 in an experimental BN green-white scheme, and SD24 No. 6242 in black-gray. (F.G. Gschwind, J.L. Ehernberger collection.)

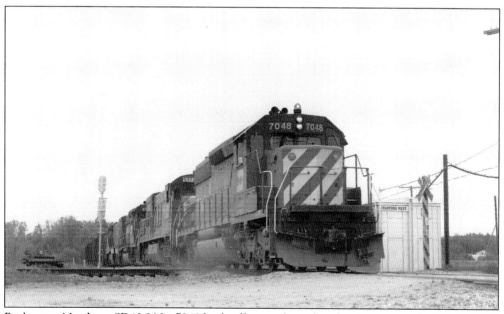

Burlington Northern SD40-2 No. 7048 leads off an eastbound coal train crossing the BN-C&NW diamond at Crawford, Nebraska, on June 10, 1978. BN traffic across the diamond was restricted to 25 miles per hour. The C&NW abandoned its line west of Crawford in 1992, eliminating this crossover. (A.J. Wolff.)

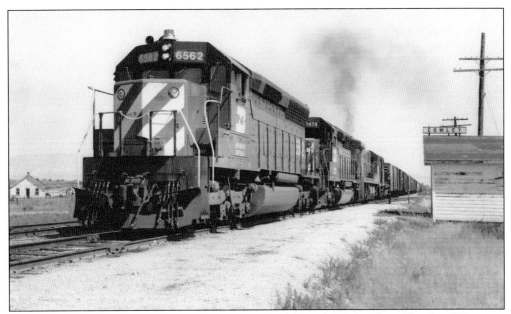

An unassuming shed with station sign greets a southbound BN freight at Cowley, Wyoming, 12 miles south of Frannie, on August 2, 1972. A pair of SD45s provide muscle on this freight assignment headed for Casper. Through freight in the BNSF era is now generally routed over the Orin line via Gillette-Guernsey. (A.J. Holck.)

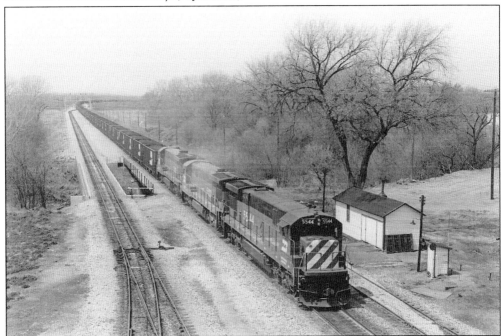

An eastbound Burlington Northern coal train arrives at Ravenna, Nebraska, on April 25, 1982, marking its departure from what was then still Alliance Division territory. Ravenna remained a terminal between the Nebraska and Alliance Divisions until Nebraska Division territory was extended to just east of Alliance (at Antioch, Nebraska) in October 1988, concurrent with abolishment of the Alliance Division. (J.J. Reisdorff.)

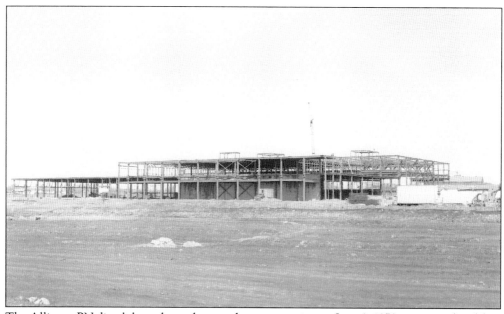

The Alliance BN diesel shop, shown here under construction on June 9, 1978, was completed four months later. A freight-car facility here opened the following January. The total shop area covers 250,000 square feet, and the facility services about 600 diesel units assigned to it. (A.J. Wolff.)

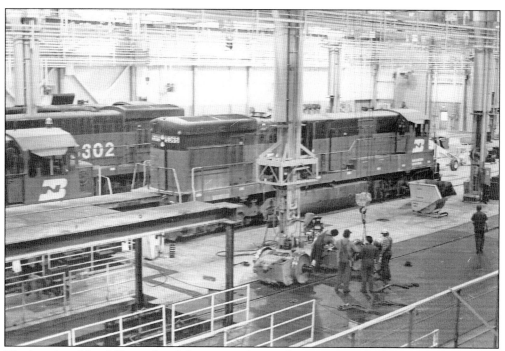

The interior of the Alliance diesel shop is seen here in January 1980. At that time, the Alliance complex was repairing an average of 22 locomotives and 70 freight cars daily. (J.J. Reisdorff.)

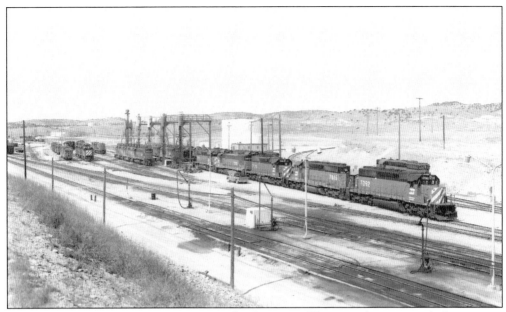

A variety of motive power was present at the Guernsey, Wyoming, locomotive fueling station on March 21, 1982. Construction of the facility began in July 1979, its location having been a former rock quarry. The facility has since been expanded and diesel storage capacity doubled to keep up with an increased demand for fueling unit coal trains. (A.J. Wolff.)

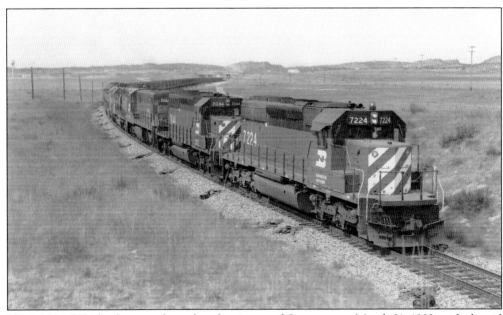

SD40-2 No. 7224 leads an eastbound coal train out of Guernsey on March 21, 1982, with the aid of three BN and three Santa Fe units. Installation of a safety signal system, called Centralized Traffic Control, was completed for Bridgeport-Sterling and Northport-Guernsey in 1981. An upgrading of the already-existing Alliance-Mullen CTC was also undertaken, completing the conversion of all coal routes to CTC. (A.J. Wolff.)

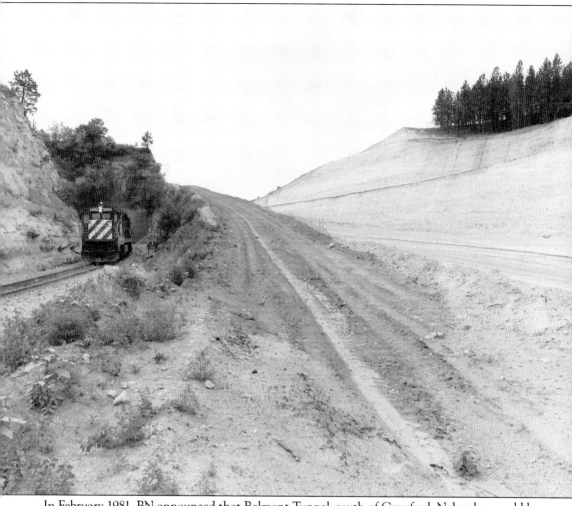

In February 1981, BN announced that Belmont Tunnel, south of Crawford, Nebraska, would be bypassed with a relocated double-track main line. When the entire $13.6 million Crawford Hill project was completed on May 3, 1982, construction crews had moved 2.2 million cubic yards of soil and rock. Here, the tunnel bypass is in progress from the north end as a BN freight passes through the old tunnel in July 1981. The last train passed through Belmont Tunnel on May 3, 1982, before a switch to the new line. Plans to remove the tunnel itself were changed so it could be preserved. The right-of-way through Belmont Tunnel now serves as a maintenance road for BNSF. (Burlington Northern, J.J. Reisdorff collection.)

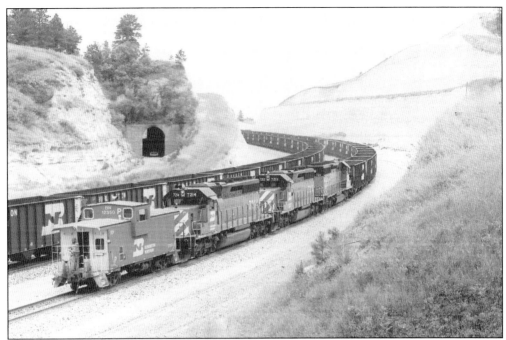

The line relocation in the vicinity of Belmont Tunnel cut 20 minutes off travel time for trains and gave Burlington Northern 37 miles of continuous double track from Marsland, Nebraska, to Joder, Wyoming. However, the 1.59-percent ruling grade remained, and helper engines stationed at Crawford, Nebraska, were still required. Here, a trio of Canadian-built SD40-2s assist an eastbound coal train past the abandoned tunnel's north portal on August 20, 1982. (Tim Zukas, J.J. Reisdorff collection.)

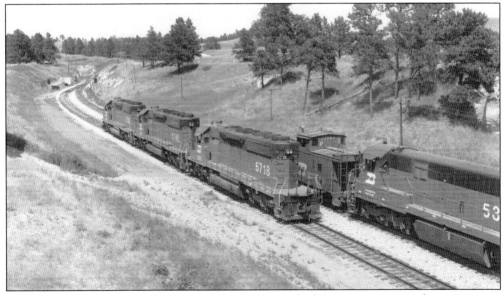

A three-unit helper waits at Belmont while another set (right) comes to a stop after assisting an eastbound coal train up Crawford Hill on July 16, 1977. The latter set, with BN 5363, will back past the switch, drop off the caboose on the fly, then couple up with the three SD40-2s for a trip back to Crawford, Nebraska. (A.J. Wolff.)

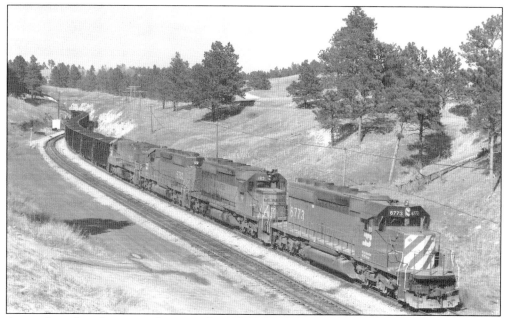

An eastbound coal train winds its way through Nebraska's Pine Ridge and the curves at Belmont on March 25, 1978. The power consist, in addition to a Milwaukee Road unit, included BN U30C No. 5383. The U30Cs were the railroad's avant-garde of coal era motive power. One such unit, the 5802 (ex-BN 5302), was later donated to an energy museum at Gillette, Wyoming. Another, the 5383, is at the Illinois Railway Museum. (A.J. Wolff.)

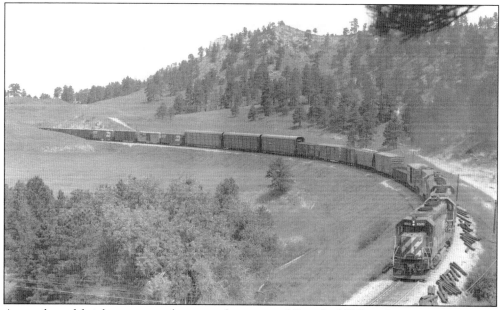

An eastbound freight moves up the west-side summit of Crawford Hill on June 10, 1978. During a 1981–1982 track reconstruction project, the sharpest curve on the Hill, at Breezy Point, the apex of Horseshoe Curve, was blunted from ten to eight degrees. (A.J. Wolff.)

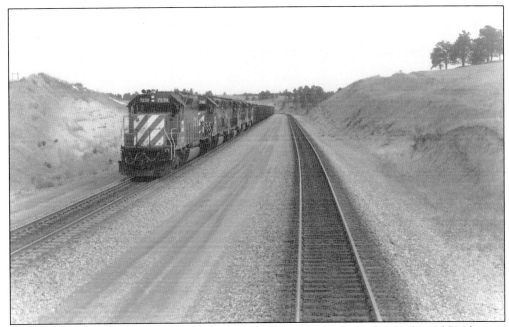

This view of Crawford Hill action in the late 1980s is from the cab of a westbound BN hopper train. Here, at 9:00 a.m. on February 25, 1989, the westbound move meets Extra 7239 East on then-new double track at milepost 411, formerly the site of Belmont Tunnel. (A.J. Pfeiffer, J.J. Reisdorff collection.)

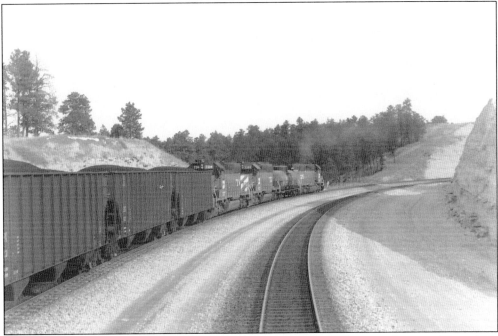

Taken in succession with the above photograph, this view shows helpers on the rear of Extra 7239 East near Belmont. At the time, three sets of helper units were stationed at Crawford, Nebraska. Note that a BN fuel tender had been added to the helper consist, a standard operating technique used at that time to reduce servicing on the units. (A.J. Pfeiffer, J.J. Reisdorff collection.)

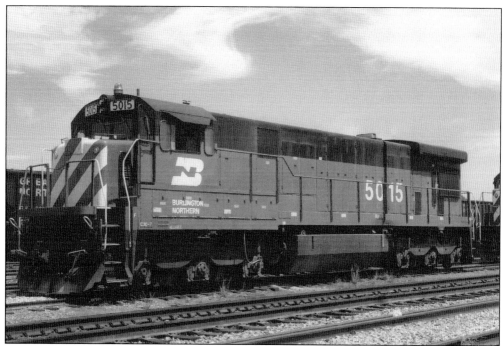

Less than a year old, C30-7 No. 5015 was one of 240 such motors purchased by Burlington Northern primarily to move the ever-increasing amount of coal being transported from Wyoming's Powder River Basin. Rated at 3,000 horsepower, five or six of these engines were required for unit coal trains west of Alliance, and three east of there. The C30-7 was the next step up from GE's U30C model. Here, BN No. 5015 awaits assignment at Guernsey, Wyoming, on July 29, 1980. (Ed Fulcomer, R.C. Kistler collection.)

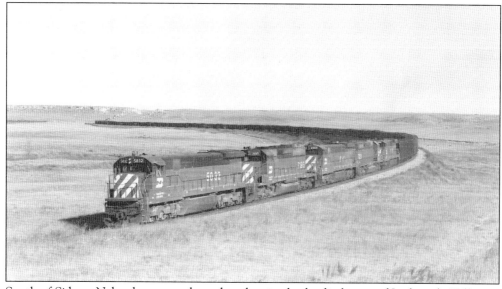

South of Sidney, Nebraska, an eastbound coal train slowly climbs out of Lodgepole Valley on January 2, 1982, using a total of 15,000 horsepower. The mix of GE and EMD units created interesting power combinations, the sounds of their exhaust under heavy load providing a dramatic effect. (A.J. Wolff.)

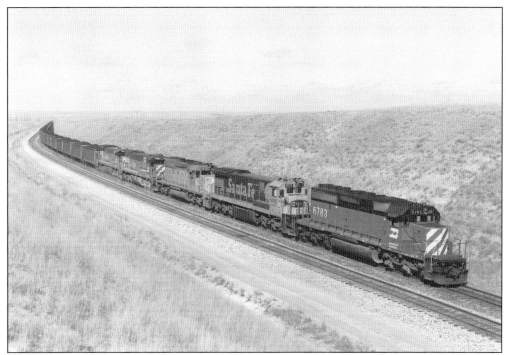

On October 10, 1987, an eastbound "coalie" at Logan, Wyoming, was hauled by power from three roads: Burlington Northern, Santa Fe, and Union Pacific. The train wheeled through barren countryside that was worth a fortune due to the bountiful supply of coal lying beneath. Between 1972 and 1985, sixteen new Western coal mines opened—all but one in the Powder River Basin. (A.J. Wolff.)

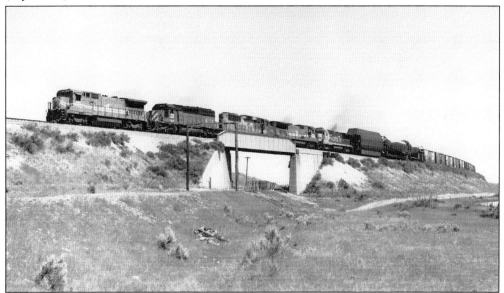

A BNSF westbound manifest freight crosses over the abandoned Chadron-Lander roadbed of the Chicago & North Western Railway on July 1, 1996, west of Orin, Wyoming. LMX motor No. 8562 leads a variety consist of four other motors. A three-car shipment from Boeing's Wichita, Kansas, plant was placed at the head end of the train, as per instruction. (A.J. Wolff.)

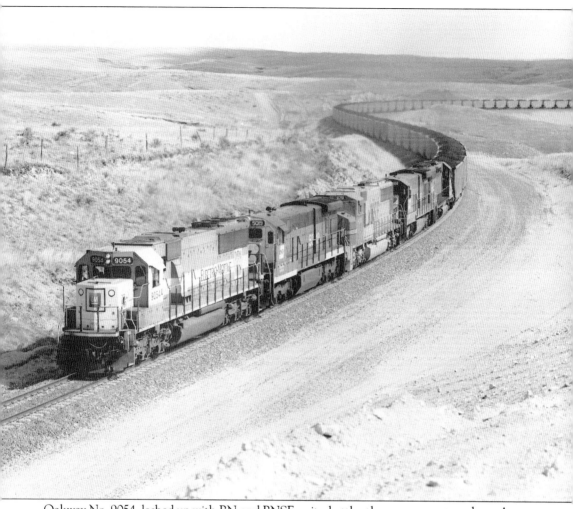

Oakway No. 9054, lashed up with BN and BNSF units, battles the one-percent grade on Angora Hill, south of Angora, Nebraska, with a KCPL (Kansas City Power & Light) coal train on April 6, 1996. Multiple unit lash-ups of modern diesel power have relegated to history the need for former helper stations like Angora. (A.J. Wolff.)

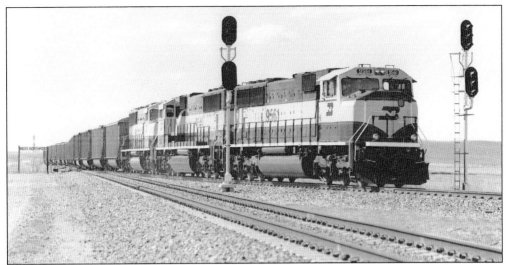

BN No. 9561 leads a trio of SD70MACs eastbound with a loaded coal train at West Northport, Nebraska, on April 14, 1995. The train is moving onto the wye leading up to Angora Hill. Northport developed into a busy junction with ever-increasing coal traffic. SD70MACs were referred to on the BN as "Grinsteins," in tribute to the company's CEO, Gerald Grinstein. (A.J. Wolff.)

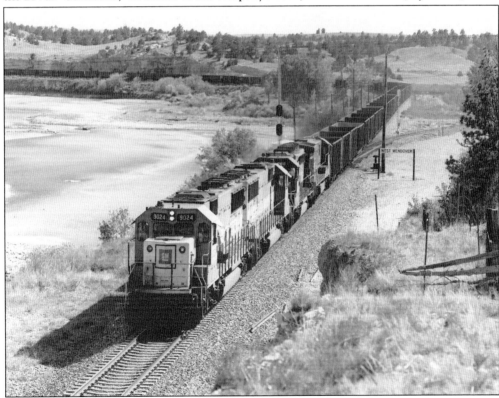

Rounding the curve at West Wendover, Wyoming, on September 27, 1992, a westbound train of empty KCPL coal hoppers heads to the mine to be reloaded. Oakway 9024 fronted a power consist with another SD60 and two BN units. The train was crossing over the switch to the west leg of the wye connecting with the former Colorado & Southern line from Denver. (A.J. Wolff.)

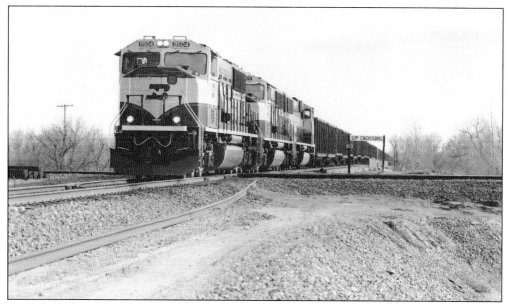

A westbound hopper train crosses over Union Pacific's O'Fallons, Nebraska, to South Torrington, Wyoming, line at Northport, Nebraska, on April 15, 1994. BN No. 9504 was built in October 1994. Similar to the additional SD70MAC units in the consist, it can serve not only for coal train service, but for general freight and grain train movements throughout the system. (A.J. Wolff.)

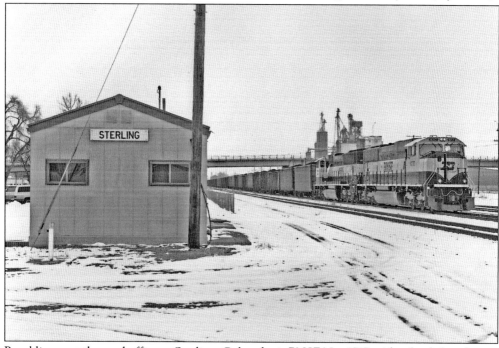

Rumbling past the yard office at Sterling, Colorado, is BNSF No. 9717 with a loaded coal train on February 12, 2000. While this subdivision sees mainly loaded and empty coal-service trains, numerous freight traffic is also handled. Interchange with Union Pacific is maintained at Sterling, while the branch line that runs east from Sterling to Holdrege, Nebraska, is now operated by a regional short line, the Nebraska-Kansas-Colorado Railway. (A.J. Wolff.)

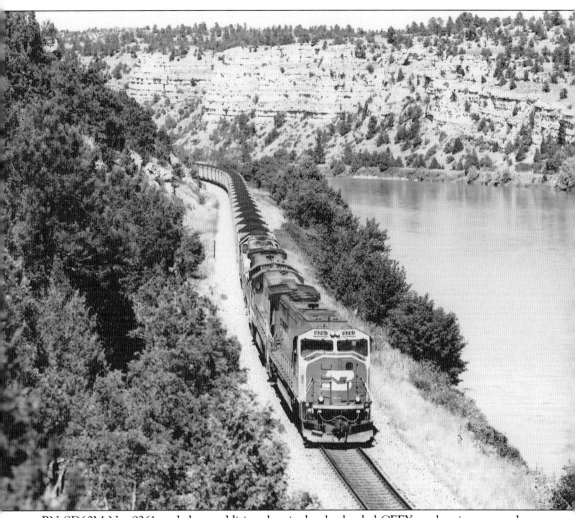

BN SD60M No. 9261 and three additional units haul a loaded CEFX coal train eastward on August 29, 1998, in a canyon adjacent to the North Platte River near Wendover, Wyoming. This scenic area, once a freight-only line in the CB&Q era, is now heavily utilized by Wyoming coal traffic. (A.J. Wolff.)

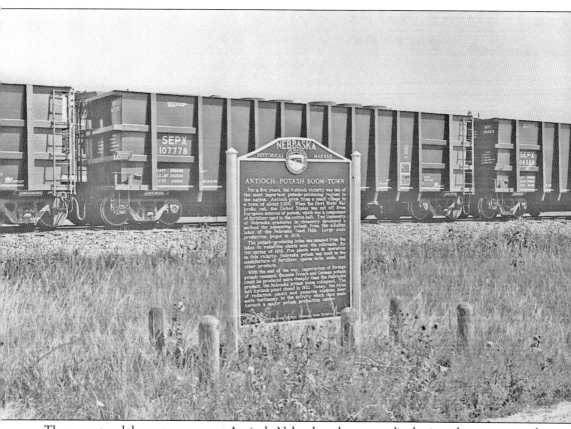

The present and the past converge at Antioch, Nebraska, where an earlier business boom associated with extracting elements from the earth had once taken place. Here, BN coal trains roll by a historical marker for the Sandhills ghost town of Antioch in August 1980. The marker memorializes the potash works that existed there from 1916 to 1921, brought on by the nation's supply of foreign potash being cut off during World War I. Potash is used in the production of fertilizer and other products. The town's population swelled to more than 2,000 during the production years. Other boom-to-bust potash facilities served by the CB&Q were located at Hoffland and Lakeside in Nebraska. (J.J. Reisdorff.)

Nine
THE BNSF ERA

Coal remained a major commodity for BNSF, just as it had for Burlington Northern. The first BNSF operating timetables, dated August 1, 1996, placed Alliance under the jurisdiction of the new Powder River Division, with superintendents of operation at both Alliance and Gillette, Wyoming. By April 1, 1998, the superintendent's office was at Alliance, although by the early 2000s, it had been moved to Denver and later to Gillette. On the busy Orin Line, shared with Union Pacific from Shawnee Junction to East Caballo Junction, Wyoming, three main tracks had been put in service over the entire 103 miles by 2007. On May 14, 2008, 21 miles of fourth main track over Logan Hill were put in service.

By March 2008, BNSF employed more than 1,600 people in Alliance and averaged about 75 trains a day, 90 percent of them servicing coal. Many employees hired in the first big expansion of the 1970s were now ready to retire. In the mechanical department, 130 new employees had been hired in the last two years, out of 750 at the Alliance shop.

However, not all of Alliance's rail traffic is coal related. Following the 1970 BN merger, additional time freights were routed via Alliance to take advantage of the new, shorter single-line routes between the Pacific Northwest and Chicago, as well as to Kansas City and St. Louis. The merger of BN with the St. Louis–San Francisco Railway in 1980 further enhanced traffic movement. BNSF operates two scheduled time freights between Kansas City, Missouri, and Pasco, Washington, traversing the Edgemont-Ravenna route. An extra east and west freight runs regularly, and, many times, solid trains of tank cars with fuel oil for the locomotive servicing facilities in Alliance are operated. Movements of Boeing jet fuselages from Wichita, Kansas, to Renton, Washington, are also regularly seen.

In recent years, the future of coal has become uncertain, with competition from natural gas and concerns about climate change. But booming oil production is now filling tank cars; oil trains are becoming regular sights, too. BNSF pioneered the modern crude-by-rail era, loading the first unit train of oil at Stanley, North Dakota, in December 2009.

It appears that the tracks of the old Alliance Division will continue to guide Alliance's engine of progress well into the future.

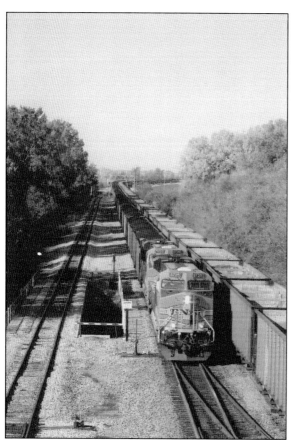

AC4400CW Nos. 5725 and 5730 are eastbound with coal loads while arriving at Ravenna, Nebraska, on October 19, 2004, as a westbound empty departs for Alliance on the Sandhills subdivision. Ravenna, a crew change point belonging to the Nebraska Division, provides lodging for crews from both divisions. By 2010, railroaders from two divisions, the Nebraska and Powder River, about 500 in all, would be working in and out of Ravenna. (David Doering.)

Traveling the Sandhills subdivision, BNSF Dash 9-44C units round a curve on the single track main near Lakeside, Nebraska, with a westbound assignment on October 18, 2006. The Sandhills, which cover northwest Nebraska, are grass-covered plains consisting of subsurface sandy soil. Although the terrain remains the same, the motive power and traffic have greatly changed since the Burlington & Missouri River Railroad first laid track through the region more than a century ago. (David Doering.)

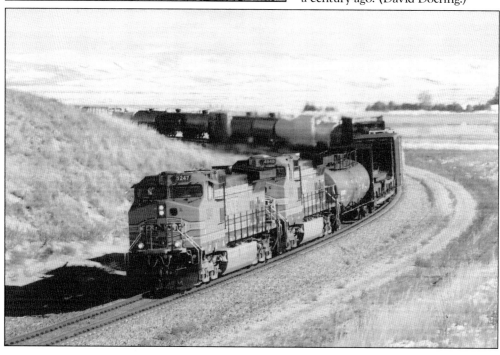

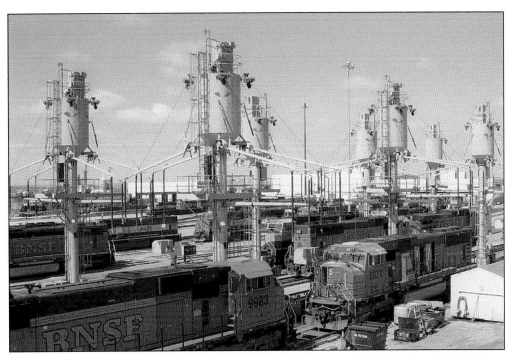

The BNSF locomotive sanding and maintenance area at Alliance is pictured on June 9, 2003. Here, locomotives are serviced with sand, water, and fuel, and inspections are done before the units are sent back into service. During this time, more than 120 units were being serviced daily, and more than 200,000 gallons of diesel fuel were being dispensed every 24 hours. (Steve Snook.)

A coal car undergoes repairs at the Alliance BNSF shop on June 10, 2003. At the time, the Alliance car shop was changing out more than 1,000 pairs of wheels monthly. Alliance also acquired two private freight-car repair facilities, both working primarily on coal hoppers. Railcar Maintenance Company is located three miles east of Alliance, and nearby is the Southwest Electric Power facility. Similar plants are now in operation at Northport, Nebraska, and Bill, Wyoming. (Steve Snook.)

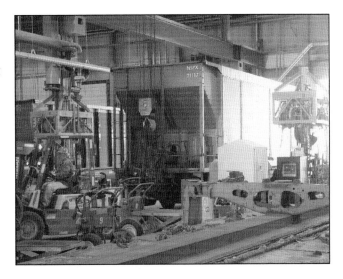

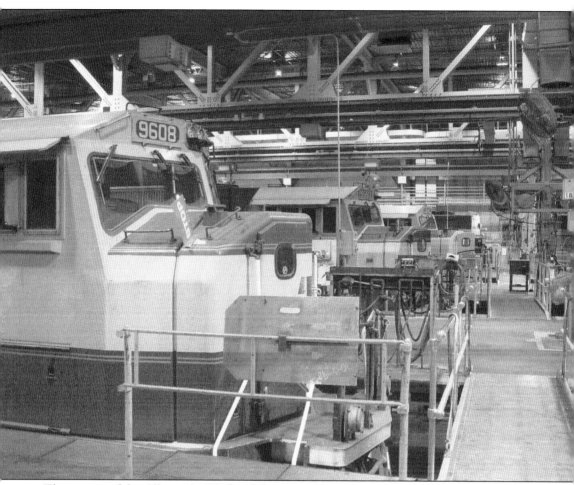

The interior of the Alliance BNSF diesel shop, seen here on June 10, 2003, shows the front ends of several locomotives, referred to by railroaders as "motors," being maintained. The main focus of the Alliance shops was for the repair of EMD-built locomotives, while the BNSF shops at Lincoln, Nebraska, handled those motors constructed by GE. Electrical and mechanical repairs are made at Alliance, including traction motor change-out and, occasionally, main generator repair. (Steve Snook.)

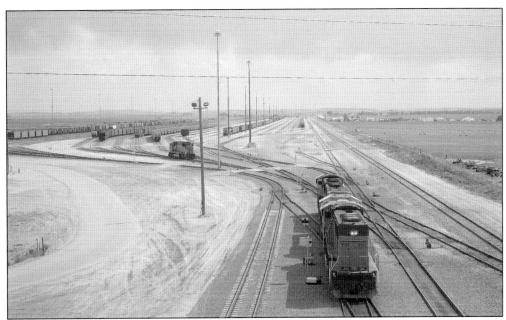

Placed into service in early 1980 was the new Alliance South Yard to support the existing, but completely remodeled, North Yard. The South Yard, seen here on June 9, 2003, serves as a major coal train service yard. Built alongside the Sterling line, it eliminated yard congestion and greatly sped up traffic flow. (Steve Snook.)

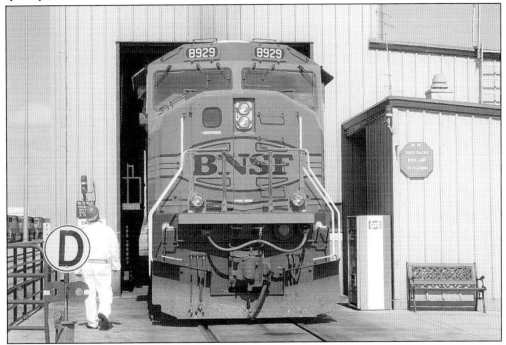

As of 2003, Alliance was the headquarters of the railroad's fleet of SD70 MAC locomotives used in coal train service. Here, on June 9, SD70MAC No. 8929 is being backed into the BNSF wash building in order for the unit to be cleaned. Locomotives are washed on an as-needed basis. (Steve Snook.)

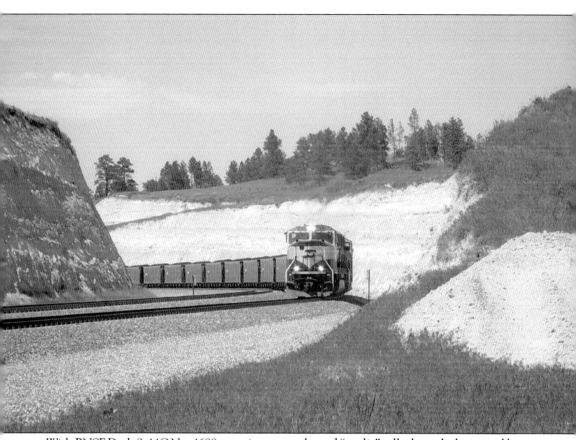

With BNSF Dash 9-44C No. 4688 on point, an eastbound "coalie" rolls through the tunnel bypass at Belmont, Nebraska, on June 10, 2003, more than 20 years after this major line relocation had been completed by predecessor Burlington Northern. Moving loads over Crawford Hill can still be as challenging as when it was done with CB&Q steam engines or BN C30-7 diesels, but major track improvements have made a difference in the overall operations. (Steve Snook.)

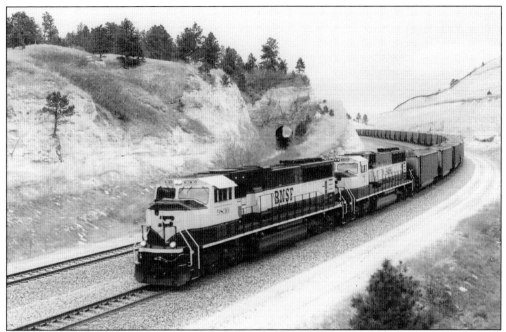

What has become one of the favorite spots for railfan photography in western Nebraska is the vicinity of the now-abandoned Belmont Tunnel. Here, BNSF No. 9890, sporting a very clean appearance, rounds a curve with a westbound empty en route to the Powder River Basin on November 9, 2000. (David Doering.)

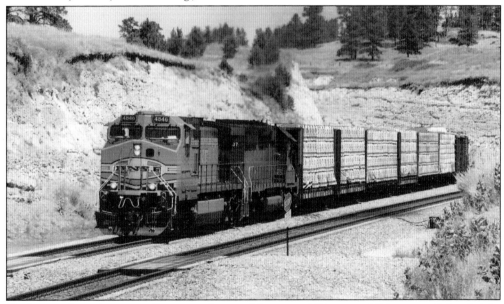

Coal is not the only commodity currently routed between Alliance and Edgemont. Other freight traffic has increased substantially. Following the 1970 BN merger, it was found that the route from the Pacific Northwest to Chicago was shorter via Alliance than via the Twin Cities, and much shorter to the Kansas City–St. Louis gateway. Coming through a cut at Belmont is an eastbound manifest on July 14, 2000. A two-year construction project installing double track and reducing sharp curves greatly improved traffic velocity in this area. (David Doering.)

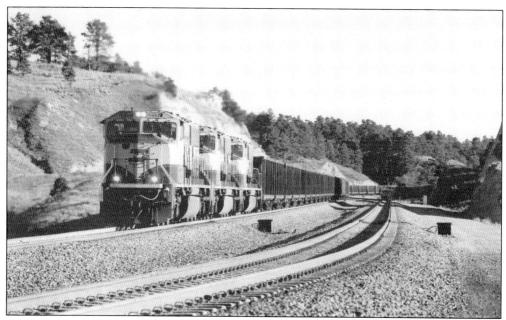

On November 5, 1999, a trio of SD70MACs is about to enter the curve at Breezy Point on Crawford Hill. Even with current diesel-electric locomotive technology, Crawford Hill still presents a challenge for eastbound tonnage trains. The stiff, 12-mile grade requires the help of pushers out of Crawford to increase available horsepower to around 25,000, all in throttle run 8, moving 17,000 tons up to Belmont. The westbound movement of empty coal trains is almost effortless in comparison. (David Doering.)

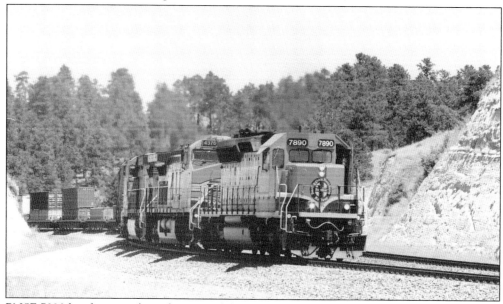

BNSF 7890 heads an eastbound intermodal over Crawford Hill on July 14, 2000. The scene is notable for 7890 having been one of two SD40-2s formerly equipped as an experimental clean-burning liquefied natural gas (LNG) locomotive. The ex-C&S motor was used in coal train service for 1991–1996, prior to BNSF replacing the prime mover with a regular power unit. Note the flared hood, a result of the LNG equipment. (David Doering.)

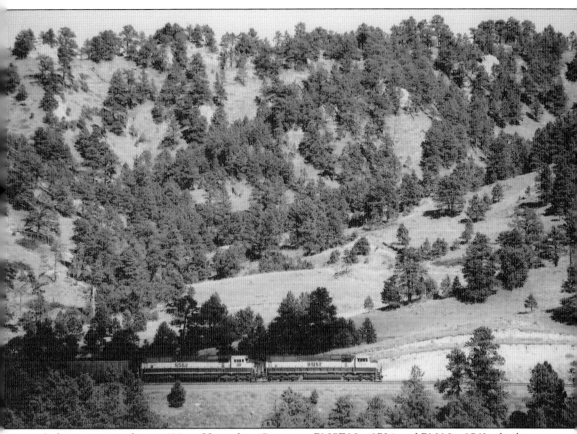

Laboring past milepost 414 on Horseshoe Curve are BNSF No. 9734 and BN No. 9562, climbing Crawford Hill in July 2000. Ahead lies Breezy Point. Compare this view with the one from the days of steam on page 22. The pine-covered hills reverberate to the heavy exhaust of each passing train—as they have done since the railroad was first built through this region. (David Doering.)

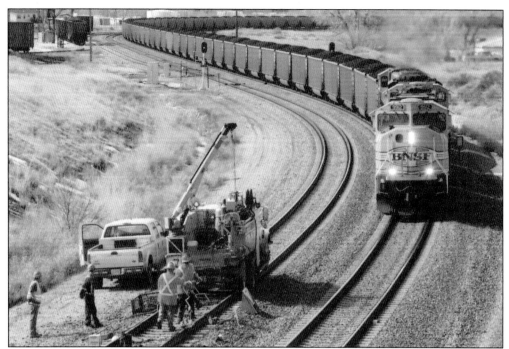

A trio of BNSF SD70MAC units rounds a curve while eastbound, past a welding crew at Newcastle, Wyoming, on March 2, 2009. Heavy traffic demands that the track be kept in excellent condition. Welding is a safe and cost-effective method to accomplish this goal. At upper left is a woodchip-loading facility. (Travis Dewitz.)

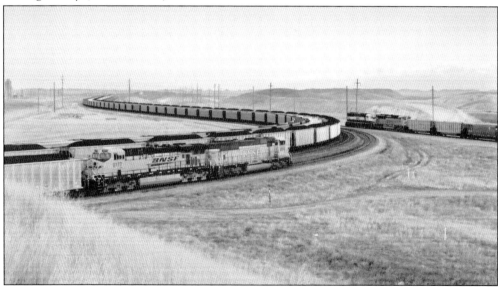

BNSF's coal train traffic originating from the Powder River Basin of Wyoming currently continues under the jurisdiction of what is now the Powder River Division. This March 3, 2009, photograph, looking west toward Reno Junction, shows the large amount of coal train traffic originating from the Black Thunder Mine in Wyoming. The train at left is pulling out of the Black Thunder Mine spur. Meanwhile, the train at right is headed for the Jacobs Ranch Mine with Distributed Power Units in place on the rear. (Travis Dewitz.)

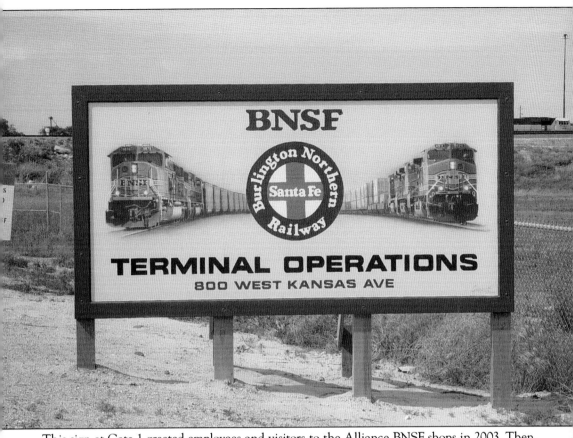

This sign at Gate 1 greeted employees and visitors to the Alliance BNSF shops in 2003. Then, five years later, the Alliance terminal was handling 70–75 trains per day on average. A record day was October 4, 2008, when 90 trains were recorded through the Alliance terminal; 42 loaded and 44 empty coal trains, and 4 freights. It is a far cry from the amount of traffic handled by an earlier generation of railroaders on the old Alliance Division. (Steve Snook.)

Discover Thousands of Local History Books Featuring Millions of Vintage Images

Arcadia Publishing, the leading local history publisher in the United States, is committed to making history accessible and meaningful through publishing books that celebrate and preserve the heritage of America's people and places.

Find more books like this at
www.arcadiapublishing.com

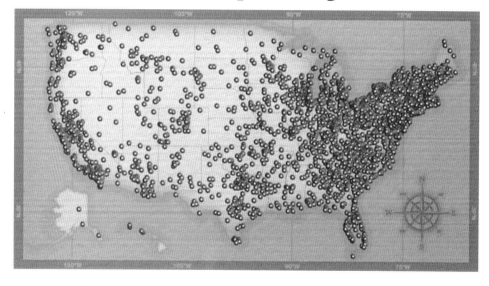

Search for your hometown history, your old stomping grounds, and even your favorite sports team.

Consistent with our mission to preserve history on a local level, this book was printed in South Carolina on American-made paper and manufactured entirely in the United States. Products carrying the accredited Forest Stewardship Council (FSC) label are printed on 100 percent FSC-certified paper.

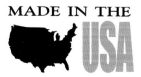